D0064483

CHANGE
the WORLD

Recovering the Message and Mission of Jesus

Mike Slaughter

Abingdon Press
Nashville

CHANGE THE WORLD
RECOVERING THE MESSAGE AND MISSION OF JESUS

Library of Congress Cataloging-in-Publication Data

Slaughter, Michael.
    Change the world : recovering the message and mission of Jesus / Mike Slaughter.
       p.   cm.
    Includes bibliographical references (p.   ).
    ISBN 978-1-4267-0297-6 (pbk. : alk. paper)
    1. Mission of the church.   I. Title.
    BV601.8.S58   2010
    269—dc22

                                                                          2009043981

10 11 12 13 14 15 16 17 18 19—10 9 8 7 6 5 4 3 2 1

MANUFACTURED IN THE UNITED STATES OF AMERICA

Praise for *Change the World*

Slaughter has long been something of a prophet, showing a holy rest-lessness with just "doing church"—because his focus is Jesus, not insti-tutional Christianity. "The true greatness of any local church is measured by how many people are serving the marginalized," he insists. That test could indeed change the world.
—Howard A. Snyder, Professor of Wesley Studies, Tyndale Seminary, Toronto

With the rich tactical experience of a longtime practitioner and the keen eye of a missional strategist, Mike writes a hard-hitting, accessible book that nails the key issues facing the Western Church at the dawn of the twenty-first century. Well worth the read.
—Alan Hirsch, Author of *The Forgotten Ways* and *Untamed,* and Founder of *Forge Mission Training Network*

In *Change the World,* Mike Slaughter urges the church to take a bold stand against not only the injustice of global poverty but the spiritual poverty that leads so many in the church today to ignore those Jesus com-manded us to serve.
—Tony P. Hall, Ambassador to the United Nations Food and Agriculture Organization

I met Mike Slaughter when he was known as a "church growth guy," and I learned a lot from him then. Now I know Mike as a "Jesus' mission guy" and I am learning even more and am inspired even more—not only through his words but also through his enthusiasm, example, and sus-tained action in some of the neediest places on earth.
—Brian D. McLaren, Author/Activist (brianmclaren.net)

Once again, Mike demonstrates innovative leadership as he challenges the Church to rethink her measures of success. Mike challenges the business-as-usual church growth models and calls the Body to be the hands and feet of Christ.
—Bob Buford, Founder, Leadership Network and Author of *Halftime* and *Finishing Well*

This is a courageous book by a humble man. When someone like Mike sounds the warning that things aren't working, we need to pay attention. He has laid aside those old attractional church-growth principles and is leading the way in teaching us how large, suburban, middle-class churches can embrace incarnational service and missional living.
—Michael Frost, Author of *ReJesus, Exiles,* and *The Shaping of Things to Come*

In honor of our first grandchild,
Elisabeth Lynne Leavitt, "Ellie"

CONTENTS

FOREWORD

This book, Mike's work, and the ministry of Ginghamsburg United Methodist Church are a rallying cry for, as Mike says, "rediscovering and reclaiming the message and mission of Jesus." I've said before that each generation of believers must decide whether their Christianity will have anything to do with Jesus. That challenge faces churches, big and small alike, across the country and the world each and every day: whether what they do, how they spend their time, and how they use their resources will have anything to do with Jesus.

In October 2008, I spent the weekend with Mike at his church. I spoke four times to his congregation and the Change the World conference. After the final session of the conference, I got to see a little bit of Mike's heart for the church. We were about to walk out of the sanctuary when he stopped me. Their worship hall was filling with homeless folks, former prostitutes, alcoholics, and drug users. It was their Saturday night recovery service. Each week hundreds of people in recovery, who would never think to darken the door of most churches, gather to worship, pray, and support one another. Mike flashed a big Midwestern pastor grin and said, "Man, if this just ain't the heart of God, I don't know what is."

Over the course of the weekend, almost one thousand conference attendees and regular churchgoers made decisions to let their hearts be broken by the things that break God's heart—in response to an "altar call" we gave after every service. Commitments ranged from getting involved with advocacy for the homeless to making a change in career. Here are a few that stuck out:

"I will become a nurse and serve underprivileged kids."

"I will begin a center for women victims of domestic violence, including legal, medical, and employment assistance."

"I want to do photography for the poor and show what is happening in the world."

"I will give hope to my students who have been homeless and support those students whose families will be without income when GM closes."

"I will consider adoption."

"I will participate in homelessness awareness on my college campus."

Commitments like these are a powerful illustration of God's people seeking to change their hearts, lives, churches, neighborhoods, cities, and the world to reflect God's own heart. Within three years of Katrina's hitting New Orleans, this church had sent more than fifty teams to work and to serve in that city. We serve a God who cares about the sex slave trade, the GM plant that is closing, the orphans waiting to be adopted, and the poor who are among us. We serve a God whose cares, concerns, and vision are broader than any of us can imagine. And the church should—no, must—reflect God's heart.

Mike's challenge is simple and direct: "Quit worrying about getting people into your church and start finding opportunities to move the people who are already there out into God's service." It is a challenge that, if we pick it up, will not only change our churches but also transform the world.

Jim Wallis

INTRODUCTION
SOMETHING'S NOT WORKING

Our research shows that many of those outside of Christianity, especially younger adults, have little trust in the Christian faith, and esteem for the lifestyle of Christ followers is quickly fading among outsiders. —David Kinnaman and Gabe Lyons

The mandate for Jesus' followers is clear. The leader of our movement defined the parameters of our mission in his inaugural message at Nazareth:

> The Spirit of the Lord is on me,
> because he has anointed me
> to proclaim good news to the poor.
> He has sent me to proclaim freedom for the prisoners
> and recovery of sight for the blind,
> to set the oppressed free,
> to proclaim the year of the Lord's favor.
>   (Luke 4:18-19, quoting Isa 61:1-2)

He has already given us the action items that will be the measures of evaluation on God's final exam:

> I was hungry and you gave me something to eat . . . thirsty and you gave me something to drink . . . a stranger and you invited me in, I needed clothes and you clothed me . . . sick and you looked after me . . . in prison and you came to visit me. . . . Truly I tell you, whatever you did for one of the least of these brothers and sisters of mine, you did for me. (Matt 25:35-40)

The gospel is good news for the poor. If it is not working to benefit the poor and oppressed, then it is not the gospel! Jesus calls his followers to a lifestyle of sacrificial mission, giving ourselves with him for God's redemptive work in the world.

I write this book during one of the most severe economic recessions since the Great Depression. I live and minister near Dayton, Ohio, which has been named by *Forbes* magazine as one of the fastest dying cities in America.[1] Our economy has been centered in the main artery of the American automobile industry. It has been called the Silicon Valley of the tool and dye shops that support the industry. What was once deemed the Gem City that gave innovative birth to the likes of aviation and the cash register has become a city of abandoned factories and empty storefronts. What an incredible opportunity to be the church!

Our church is feeding more than fifteen hundred families a week through our food pantries and serving people through our gently used clothing stores and car ministry. We have a warehouse filled with hospital equipment that is loaned to any with a need who are without insurance or resources. Our GED program allows people to compete for jobs that are above the subsistence level, especially when it allows students to matriculate to the local community college and job training programs. In decaying, at-risk sections of the city, we are restarting churches that had become fortresses for the few "saints" still driving in from the suburbs, yet were walled off from the community in which they stood. We are partnering with the elementary schools in these communities with hundreds of volunteers. The results in the improvement of student test scores are truly amazing. Our Clubhouse after-school programs work with at-risk children using teen mentors who tutor in schoolwork, character, faith, and leadership.

Dayton, Ohio, is by no means unique in this economic malaise. Cincinnati, Chicago, Indianapolis, Las Vegas, and Detroit are just a few of the other cities that have been named in the *Forbes* report as being among the "emptiest US cities."[2] What an opportunity for the church to be the church—for the world to get to see the church as an active verb! But . . .

Something Is Not Working

George Barna's book *Revolution* first caught my attention in 2005. He made the disturbing prediction that the church would lose half of its market share by 2015. A 50 percent drop in participation in ten years! Other sources followed with equally dire projections. David Kinnaman and Gabe Lyons's work, *Unchristian: What a New Generation Really Thinks about Christianity*, should be a jolting wake-up call for the church.

Kinnaman and Lyons said, "The image of the Christian faith has suffered a major setback. Our most recent data show that young outsiders have lost much of their respect for the Christian faith. These days nearly two out of every five young outsiders (38 percent) claim to have a bad impression of present-day Christianity." The research reveals that the three most widely held perceptions of the Christian church are that it is (1) antihomosexual (an image held by 91 percent of sixteen- to nineteen-year-old outsiders); (2) judgmental (87 percent); and (3) hypocritical (85 percent).[3]

Survey results from Trinity College in Hartford, Connecticut, indicated that in 2009, 75 percent of Americans called themselves Christians, down from 86 percent in 1990.[4] From all indicators it is obvious that a growing number of people are becoming disenchanted with conventional church. According to Barna research, the eighteen- to thirty-five-year-olds' top three responses perceive the church to be judgmental, hypocritical, and antihomosexual.[5] Many others who have tried the church and left have experienced it to be self-serving, rigidly institutional, and neither relational nor relevant.

I asked people on Facebook: "Why do you feel the church is not working for the majority of people?" My informal survey prompted responses like these:

"The Church lacks a message of hope."
"Lives that contradict teachings."
"Teaching that is abstract and not relevant to daily living."
"I feel that I will be judged and condemned if I go to church."
"Pastors who make poor choices in their personal lives."

"Christians look down on those who fail to live up to their standards."

"The common thread in the reasons my friends avoid church is hypocrisy."

"I haven't found any churches that are engaging. They seem to be all about rituals and never relevant to today."

"I feel that I am being talked at, never as a participant but as an observer."

"Churches fail to address the life issues of college age students in a time when we are questioning faith."

One respondent gave these reasons why her church worked:

"What I love about my church is that we seem to reach all levels of society! I don't feel condemned when I come to church. I leave wanting to be a better person and wanting to change this world to be a better place for my children. I leave feeling equipped with the right tools to be the hands and feet of Jesus."

Mainline churches have been in a state of decline since the 1970s. My own denomination (The United Methodist Church) bears an eerie resemblance to the anemic American automobile industry. As of the spring of 2009, General Motors was down 51 percent in market share since 1960. (GM later declared bankruptcy in June of 2009.) In that same period the UMC was down 52 percent. We lost 365,000 members between 2001 and 2007. In that six-year period, worship attendance declined by 8.5 percent, and the number of members received by profession of faith was down 18 percent. If the UMC continues in this patterned trend, there will be no one left by 2050.[6]

The megachurch phenomenon of the 1980s and 1990s seemed to offer hope for the dawn of a new awakening. In 1992 there were less than 100 churches with 2,000 or more in attendance throughout North America. That number had grown to more than 1,250 in 2005.[7] But a September 2008 USA Today article reported that growth had stalled in megachurches. Willow Creek Community, Saddleback, and Lakewood, three of the largest attendance churches in America, experienced attendance declines in 2007. This is a growing trend reported among many churches that were tracking yearly positive gains throughout the last two decades. What worked—or we thought was working—is no longer working with the sixteen- to thirty-five-year-olds of today.

Faulty Measures

The measures of success for the rapidly growing churches of the last two decades tended to focus on the ABCs of church growth: attendance, buildings, cash.

How many churches record weekly attendance and monetary offerings in their bulletins? We turn in reports and measure our identities based on the size of attendance and membership. Maybe a little too much like the sin committed by King David when he became overly consumed with numbers and census taking (2 Sam 24). The never-ending building campaign for the growing church diverts critical resources away from meeting the needs of the least and lost. As church campuses expand, the cost of maintenance and utilities escalates. Less of our monies and energies go for those things that are closest to the heart of God. There must be a better way!

I have served Ginghamsburg Church for more than thirty years now. I have seen it grow from fewer than 100 people in a rural small town setting to almost 5,000 people worshiping on our three Dayton campuses and in numerous house churches each week. I cut my ministry teeth influenced by the church growth movement. I went to all of the seminars, breaking the 200 barrier, the 400 barrier, and so on. We mastered seeker-sensitive worship and practiced innovation in worship arts. We were one of the early pioneers in media ministry. We bought 130 acres to build what we facetiously called the "Disney World" campus. One architect who worked on the Orlando theme park was hired to create a long-range plan for our acreage. A plan was developed for a 3,000-seat sanctuary. However, it was never built, and we no longer have plans to do so.

As I enthusiastically challenged our people forward, I experienced a discomfort in my spirit and began to question my former measures of success. We had achieved getting behinds in the seats, but I realized that all we had really done was accumulate crowds of spectators who were not moving toward deeper faith and service.

Many people in our churches today profess faith in God, but they embody the values of the dominant culture. They possess a soft-secular worldview rather than the worldview of Jesus. These folks believe in God and profess Jesus, but they trust the materialistic values of secular culture. They have bought into the materialistic lie that has led to the financial precipice on which the world teeters today. Consider, for example, that by 2005, Americans had reached a negative savings rate, spending $1.22 for every $1.00 earned.

Church, we have met the enemy and it is *us*!

Since that "conversion" in my leadership in the late 1990s, I have longed to spend the second half of my ministry being and doing the things that mattered most to God.[8] I didn't want to give one more year to things like building campaigns that diverted much-needed resources and energy from the most urgent human situations. I wanted to become Christ's advocate against the demonic atrocities that obliterate human spirit.

Since 2005, Ginghamsburg Church (with our strategic partner UMCOR—the United Methodist Committee on Relief) has built more than 150 schools, trained more than 200 teachers, and created a sustainable agricultural program that is feeding close to 80,000 people and building water yards that will serve more than 200,000 people and their livestock in Darfur. The Darfur region of Sudan is the location of the first genocide of the twenty-first century. The United Nations has called it the worst humanitarian crisis in the world. There is a better Way, and it is Jesus' way!

Biblical Measures

In this book, I have attempted to challenge many of our current church traditions and paradigms that we have falsely canonized as biblical truth. The religious scholars of Jesus' day regarded his hermeneutic as heretical. Our faith practice has also become a distortion of Jesus' gospel of the kingdom of God. We often embrace a disembodied "saved for heaven" theology. We have overemphasized getting people into heaven to the neglect of getting heaven into earth. True church growth is not about how many people attend each weekend. The true greatness of any local church is measured by how many people serve the marginalized. Jesus had a church of only 120 members when he left planet earth. By most church growth standards, this membership would be deemed utter failure. But Jesus used a very different measure. To Jesus, the church was an active verb and not a passive noun. His followers practiced mission evangelism. They understood that the mission was not to get the world into the church but to get the church into the world!

The business of the church is to engage and empower disciples of Jesus in meeting the needs and closing the gaps of disparities for the least of these. The world will see the relevancy of the gospel when the people of Jesus fully embrace and live the biblical mandate to love like Jesus. John Wesley called it the demonstration of "social holiness." The church too often suffers from a numbers neurosis. Let's quit worrying about numbers in the pews and begin to be the hands and feet of Jesus in our homes, our communities, and the outermost places of the world. It is time for the church to rediscover and reclaim the message and mission of Jesus!

CHAPTER ONE

MISSIONAL VS. ATTRACTIONAL

All great missionary movements begin at the fringes of the church, among the poor and the marginalized, and seldom, if ever, at the center. —Alan Hirsch

The seeker model practiced by so many of our churches in the last few decades unintentionally lowered the bar on what it means to make the radical commitment to become a Jesus follower. Some of our superficial theology is the residue of evangelistic methodologies that sold grace at wholesale prices. We cajole people into making decisions for Jesus rather than truthfully challenge people to calculate the cost of following Jesus in a lifestyle of sacrificial service. We invite the uninitiated to become members of a movement they don't even understand without clearly laying out the expectations of the movement's revolutionary leader.

There has been a growing restlessness in the church during the first decade of the twenty-first century. The models of the last decades of the twentieth century are no longer adequate to address the questions and needs of younger generations. Many of those who are disenchanted with the church, however, have a more positive image of Jesus. Their experience and understanding of the church are counter to the Jesus of their expectation. We in the church are

we're got to show them Jesus

1

perceived as being very unlike Jesus in our priorities, attitudes, politics, and lifestyles. The emergent movement has grown out of this disenchantment by those who are part of the church but feel that the church has neglected Jesus' emphasis on the kingdom of God and its redemptive influence in the world. The proponents of this movement rightly emphasize the Messiah of Isaiah who will bring God's justice and righteousness to the poor and marginalized. Others in the church refer to the emerging influences as "missional church," which emphasizes the attempt to reconnect to the apostolic DNA of the original movement. (Authors Michael Frost and Alan Hirsch are proponents of this perspective.) The missional church is actively moving out and engaging the world in the places of greatest need rather than marketing the world into the church. I refer to this throughout the book as rediscovering and reclaiming the message and mission of Jesus.

The Kingdom on Earth

The Jewish people of Jesus' day were expectantly awaiting the dawn of the messianic kingdom. The prophet Isaiah foretold "the year of the LORD's favor." Jesus read from this passage in his inaugural message in his hometown of Nazareth:

> The Spirit of the Sovereign LORD is on me . . .
> to proclaim good news to the poor.
> He has sent me to bind up the brokenhearted,
> to proclaim freedom for the captives
> and release from darkness for the prisoners,
> to proclaim the year of the LORD's favor . . .
> to comfort all who mourn,
> and provide for those who grieve in Zion. (Isa 61:1-3)

This expectant kingdom was not a disembodied heaven that people would ascend to in the afterlife but a righting or restoration of God's created order on earth. Isaiah stated,

> They will rebuild the ancient ruins
> and restore the places long devastated;
> they will renew the ruined cities
> that have been devastated for generations. (v. 4)

Jesus proclaimed the arrival of this new kingdom order. His message was clearly focused on the kingdom of God's present influence in the world rather than on going to heaven when we die. Rather, heaven has come to earth, or as Jesus said in the Gospel of Mark, "The kingdom of God has come near. Repent and believe the good news!" (1:15).

From his prison cell, John sent word to Jesus asking if he was truly the one who had been promised through the centuries by the ancient prophets or "should we expect someone else?" (Luke 7:18-19). Jesus did not go into a theological discourse but pointed to the physical evidence of the presence of the power of God to complete the works of God: "Go back and report to John what you have seen and heard: The blind receive sight, the lame walk, those who have leprosy are cleansed, the deaf hear, the dead are raised, and the good news is proclaimed to the poor" (Luke 7:22). Jesus claimed to be the long-awaited Messiah whose presence would signify the presence of God's kingdom and the restoration of all things. The evidence of his claims was not in his words but was demonstrated through the fruit of God's works. After he read the passage announcing the messianic presence (Isa 61) in the synagogue in Nazareth, he dropped the big bombshell: "Today this scripture is fulfilled in your hearing" (Luke 4:21). The evidence was the direct intervention of God's heart and healing purpose in the lives of the poor and broken. The people of the messianic kingdom don't escape from the world's diseased brokenness but engage the world and all those in it at the greatest places of need. Jesus followers are not waiting for heaven but are actively rebuilding, restoring, and renewing the lives of broken people and the shattered communities of despair. Yes, we are waiting for the return of the King. But it is not passive waiting!

The church described in the book of Acts (notice that the book is named Acts and not Doctrines) was continually moving beyond all institutional walls and doctrines to faithfully demonstrate the good news of the Kingdom. It was a major deal for Peter to move beyond the Jewish laws of defilement to include "unclean Gentiles." And the church was not beyond the frailties of divisions. We could say that the first church split was the denominational formation of a Jewish church and a Gentile church. But we read about a visible sacrificial lifestyle that demonstrated a radically different core value. The believers embraced a countercultural lifestyle that caused those outside the church to pay serious attention:

> All the believers were together and had everything in common. They sold property and possessions to give to anyone who had need. Every day they continued to meet together in the temple courts. They broke bread in their homes and ate together with glad and sincere hearts, praising God and enjoying the favor of all the people. And the Lord added to their number daily those who were being saved. (Acts 2:44-47)

They were being a visible expression of God's right-side-up values in an upside-down world.

Who we are and why we are here are realized as we live and serve God together in community under the authority of the Lord Jesus Christ. The values of this community are not established by trends in media, arts, politics, or economics. Those values change with every generation. The values of the kingdom of God are eternal.

Ministry with the Poor

> Listen, my dear brothers and sisters: Has not God chosen those who are poor in the eyes of the world to be rich in faith and to inherit the kingdom he promised those who love him? But you have dishonored the poor. Is it not the rich who are exploiting you? Are they not the ones who are dragging you into court? Are they not the ones who are blaspheming the noble name to whom you belong? (James 2:5-7)

Our churches reflect the economic homogeneity of our culture more than they do the priorities of the kingdom. James pointed to the fact that we are guilty of economic favoritism. How many people in your church think like you, vote like you, and have been nurtured in a similar economic value system? Our churches more frequently resemble exclusive fraternal organizations than they do the body of Christ. How do we determine and assign human worth? The world makes this determination based on what people have (for example, education, money, position, influence). In the kingdom of God people have value because of who they are, children created in God's image.

Most of the poverty in the world is not the result of initiative or the lack thereof. For two-thirds of the world's population, poverty is the consequence of latitude and longitude. Bono of U2 fame said that the determination of whether a person lives or dies should not depend on the accident of latitude and longitude. You are not more valued because you have been born in a first world economy with all of the luxuries it affords. Romans 2:11 reminds us that "God does not show favoritism." Why then does the Bible give such priority to the poor? Jesus affirmed this priority in the parable of the Great Banquet (Luke 14:15-24). Who ultimately becomes God's guests at the party? Invite "the poor, the crippled, the blind and the lame."

Every parent is guilty of showing favoritism at times to one child over the other. Which child can appear to get the most attention from a parent? It is often the one who is struggling the most or most troubled at the time. One of our children is most like me. She is strong willed and determined. Those years between eleventh grade and her sophomore year in college were challenging, to say the least. Our son is more like his mother. He was very obedient and never really rebelled. Just because Kristen had our intense focus didn't mean that we loved her more or less than her brother. For a time she simply required more focused attention.

There is a growing gap between the rich and the poor. The global economic crisis that began in 2008 has only accelerated the erosion of the middle class. My hometown newspaper reported that Dayton, Ohio, lost 33,000 jobs in manufacturing between 2000 and the summer of 2008. The median income in our area dropped 10.5 percent in one decade. The poverty rate in Dayton for children ages five to seventeen was 24 percent in 2000 and 32.8 percent in 2005.[1] What an opportunity for the church to rebuild, restore, and renew in devastated places! This is a time not for retreat but for engagement! Out of the 2.2 billion children in the world, 1 billion are living in poverty.[2] That is nearly half of the world's children! This is why Ginghamsburg Church and our partner churches are actively working in Darfur. Since 2005, we have invested more than $4 million in agriculture, child protection and development, and safe water projects. These funds come primarily from hardworking blue-collar folks who are living simply and sacrificially in one of America's fastest dying cities. We are restarting inner-city churches that had ceased to be relevant to the needs of the communities in which they stood. We are seeing vibrant growth in these restarts that are now reaching and serving the working poor and homeless. Our nonprofit ministries are working to engage, encourage, and empower for life and employment.

Poverty of the body can be fixed. There is a deeper level of poverty that has eternal consequences, however: poverty of the spirit. A medieval sage bluntly stated, "The want of goods is easily repaired, but the poverty of the soul is irreparable" (Montaigne, 1533–1592). Those of us in the church have been guilty of creating a gospel that is self-serving and other-judging. We spend our resources and energies on building structures and creating programs for ourselves, and then call it mission! In the name of Jesus we have idolized earthly valuables over kingdom values. Like the rich man who walked past Lazarus, we have become callous, indifferent, and insulated from the needs of our brothers and sisters lying at our doorstep. Church, we need to lose our sense of self-importance and remember: "Not many of you were wise by human standards; not many were influential; not many were of noble birth. But God chose the foolish things of the world to shame the wise; God chose the weak things of the world to shame the strong" (1 Cor 1:26-27).

We are facing challenging times. This is not a time to fear or to insulate ourselves from the human pain and suffering around us. If the world is ever going to take the good news of the gospel seriously, then we must take a serious look at our paradigms for ministry, repent, and realign our priorities and resources with the message and mission of Jesus.

The Shift: To Missional Evangelism from Attractional Evangelism

The predominant methodologies that drove strategic planning and programming during the height of the church growth-seeker era were based in "attractional" evangelism. The mantra was "build it and they will come." We built quality programming for every age and life stage. It was well targeted to meet the needs of the young baby boomers and their growing families. The church mastered slick marketing campaigns that scratched the itches of the "me generation." We built buildings that resembled the shopping malls they frequented and pioneered contemporary worship styles that rivaled the bars from their college days. The megachurch became the idolized model of success, and numbers in the pews, the measure of effectiveness. But somehow in the cycles of programming, capital campaigns, concerts, and Bible studies we forgot an important truth: curious crowds don't equal committed disciples. Many of us in our well-intentioned efforts had done well in attracting crowds who were bringing Jesus into their soft-secular worldviews instead of being transformed into his. We thought it was working, yet all the while the church as a whole continued to decline at escalating rates. And many who had come into the church continued to worship at the altar of self-indulgence, materialism, and indifference to the poor and marginalized.

The church must make a major paradigm shift from attraction evangelism to mission evangelism. In simplest terms, this is what Jesus meant when he said that all people would see that we were his disciples through the demonstration of our sacrificial love.

Attractional evangelism parallels the marketing strategy of a vacation cruise line. A cruise ship is a self-contained fortress of programming for every age and interest. The Disney World architect who Ginghamsburg hired in the mid-1990s drew up a long-range plan for our 130 acres. The design was complete with a Market Square, lake, and conference center–retreat hotel—sound familiar? Have you ever been on a cruise? The experience is intensely planned and organized. It has a hierarchical staff-driven structure (captain and crew). A cruise is a hedonistic experience of extravagance and excess. Okay, so maybe I have never been on one, but my parents have gone on thirteen cruises in the last ten years. I feel vicariously bloated every time my dad talks about the buffets.

People choose a cruise for the experience of vacation and retreat. You expect to be served. After all, no one leaves a mint on your pillow in the evening or makes your bed in the morning when you are home. You work so hard all the other weeks of the year. You deserve to be pampered! Go on, get the massage! On a cruise your involvement is totally based on self-interest. You can select from a seemingly endless menu of activities. Explore the interior of a mystical tropical island, whale watch among the glaciers, or swim with the dolphins. Lie on a beach or snorkel among the plethora of exotic fish along a living coral reef. If you prefer, you never need to leave the boat. Rock climbing, golf lessons, theaters, bowling alleys, and swimming pools are just a few of the opportunities that invite your time.

Who are the customers that become the focus of resources and programming for the cruise line? They are the people who pay money to be on the inside of the ship. Any wagers on the income levels and ages of those who choose to take cruises? I guarantee it is not the poor and marginalized! And why is it that the majority of people who frequently cruise seem to be more closely aligned with my parents' generation? Do you see any similarities with the mainline church?

Mission evangelism, on the other hand, parallels the priorities and focus of a mission outpost in a challenging place of great human need. Unlike the self-contained programming model that has been practiced by many growing churches in the past, the mission model depends on networking. The missional church is actively creating partnerships with social agencies, public schools, government and nongovernment organizations, as well as other faith groups.

MISSIONAL VS. ATTRACTIONAL

MISSIONAL PARTNERSHIPS

Ginghamsburg's work in Darfur can only happen because of the strategic partners with which we have networked. UMCOR (United Methodist Committee On Relief) has been the engineering/staffing partner in this project that will eventually impact close to a quarter of a million people.

Other churches, schools, and businesses have also made significant contributions. North College Hill Public Schools in Cincinnati, Ohio, have raised $25,000 and continue to make this humanitarian crisis a priority. Thomas Beckette is the pastor at Bald Knob United Methodist Church in Wharton, West Virginia, where you can find twelve to fourteen people worshiping on any given week. Pastor Tom and his people understand that the strength and vitality of any church is not measured in numbers but in members' willingness to sacrificially be the hands and feet of Jesus in the world. They contributed $1,375 in just one Christmas miracle offering for the Sudan Project (www.thesudanproject.org). Pastor John Daniels's congregation at Urbana United Methodist Church in Urbana, Ohio, which averages about 300 in worship each week, has contributed $74,251.72 to our project in the last two years. A Jewish business owner from Michigan drove six and a half hours round trip for an informational meeting about our project in Darfur. "I can't wait to get back and tell my rabbi about my involvement with Ginghamsburg Church." He sent a check for almost $20,000.

Missional churches are creating strategic partnerships and developing alternative sources of funding. Ginghamsburg's food pantries serve over 1,500 people each week and feed another 1,000 in weekly fellowship meals. We have enlisted the support of foundation grants and government agencies. You don't have to be a megachurch to feed the hungry. We started a food pantry and gently used clothing store when we had fewer than 100 people. We partnered with other churches and community organizations to assist in these embryonic endeavors. As he did with the loaves and fishes, Jesus takes our meager offerings and multiplies the miracle!

Similar to cruise ship programming, attraction evangelism is intensely planned and organized, it is staff driven, and it can tend toward extravagance and excess. Mission evangelism (like the mission outpost), on the other hand, is experimental and flexible. Like Lewis and Clark mapping an uncharted route to the West, missional churches plan and resource as they go. Catholic theologian Hans Kung put it this way: "A Church which pitches its tents without constantly looking out for new horizons, which does not continually strike camp, is being untrue to its calling. . . . [We must] play down our longing for certainty, accept what is risky, and live by improvisation and experiment."[3]

The attraction model is deficient and inefficient in its over-dependence on professional staff. The mission model is unlimited in the scope of outreach based on the commitment and passion of unpaid servants. (I prefer to use the term *servants* instead of *volunteers* because volunteers serve at their own convenience while servants serve at the discretion of the one who calls.) The rehabilitation work that continues along the Gulf Coast is a powerful example of the unrealized potential of unpaid servants. More than 90 percent of all of the work being done in the aftermath of Hurricane Katrina in New Orleans is being done by faith-based organizations.

Ginghamsburg Church has partnered with an organization in Atlanta, American Caribbean Experience, to send volunteer medical teams and business leaders to Jamaica four to six times a year. Doctors, dentists, nurses, pharmacists, and business leaders choose to give up their time and resources, multiple times in a year, for the opportunity to serve people through our clinics and microbusiness. Dr. Steve Guy is a gynecologist from the Dayton, Ohio, area who started the medical clinics on the northeastern side of the island. He recruited Dr. Mark Bentley, who just so happens to be my family's dentist, to start the dental clinics. They hold these clinics every three months in partnership with local Jamaican churches. Most are held in the sanctuaries and classrooms of the churches. Steve invited Jim Taylor, a local car dealer, to travel with them to explore the possibility of working with small business owners for training in best business practices and setting up a network for the creation of microbusiness loans. Jim already had experience in this area doing short-term mission work in Cambodia. Jim invited businessman Carey Smith to join him on his second trip, and the microloan mission was soon in full swing. These four Jesus followers are moving beyond the walls and boundaries of attraction church and believe they can change an island one life at a time. These men regularly meet together as a mission cell group for the purpose of dreaming, developing, and deploying God's dreams. They encourage and pray for one another and hold one another accountable through the study and discussion of God's word.

Steve, Mark, Jim, and Carey invited me to go with them to Port Maria, Jamaica, to experience firsthand the fruit of their "unpaid servant" labor. Traveling by car along the coast, we arrived at this Caribbean port (population 7,000 to 8,000), which is about two hours east of Montego Bay. Port Maria has none of the glitz or glamour of the tourist fortresses on the island. It truly reflects a country that hovers at or above 70 percent unemployment. Spanish settlers first settled the town as the capital of St. Mary Parish. The parish (population 113,000) is one of the poorest in Jamaica. The terrain is mountainous, rising to 4,000 feet at the highest point. The principal products are bananas, sugar, citrus, pimento, cocoa, coconuts, coffee, vegetables, and breadfruit. One of the greatest challenges for the farmers is the transportation cost of getting their produce to market. The distance and terrain make it next to impossible for the poor farmers who lack motorized transportation to get their products to market. This allows the middlemen, who take 75 percent of the producers' profits for transportation services, to victimize the farmers. A microloan of $4,000 for a truck changes the entire scenario.

Carey took me to meet one of the microloan recipients. We met on the beach in downtown Port Maria. Jermaine is a thirty-two-year-old fisherman who has made his living out of a simple elongated wooden boat since his early teen years. It is a model that has been used for centuries, with a small, well-worn outboard motor as the only recognizable sign of modernity. Jermaine has three children—two sons and a daughter—and number four is on the way. His mother died when he was seven. He was sent to live with his father, a police officer on the other side of the island, who then sent him to live with a grandfather who died shortly thereafter. Jermaine was homeless and living on the beach before he was thirteen. Local fishermen befriended him and started teaching him how to fish. Tragically, an elder that Jermaine felt closest to was murdered on the beach. Jermaine continued to fish, and when he turned eighteen, he decided that he needed a more permanent residence. He collected floating debris and pieces of wood from the sea to build the simple shack where he and his family currently reside, just a stone's throw from where we stood on the beach.

Jermaine is illiterate. He never had the means or encouragement to attend school. In Jamaica you must have shoes and the money to purchase a uniform, but Jermaine had neither. Like a majority of parents, Jermaine wants to improve the lot of his children. "I don't want any of my kids to ever have to fish!" he says. His dreams are for his daughter to be a nurse or public official and for his sons to be pilots. Carey and Jim's microloan mission made an initial loan of $400 to Jermaine after they worked with him on the development of a business plan. He used the money to do work on his boat and overhaul the motor. Part of the business plan was the addition of a tourist dimension for his business by using his boat to take tourists across the bay to a small island and out to a reef for snorkeling. Jermaine paid back the 5 percent-interest loan on time. As we stood on the beach, Jermaine was presenting a second business plan for a new loan of $500. This loan would allow Jermaine to purchase ten fish traps that would be working for him while he was running the tourist side of the business. With them he would immediately increase his production, which would increase his revenue flow by growing his customer base with the local hotels. The next phase of his business plan would allow him to employ a few friends and family members. Jermaine's business plan showed that with financial assistance he could touch the lives of twenty people.

Before we left the beach, Jermaine asked if we would like to see his home. The house is a two-room structure that fails to hide the mishmash of its origin. Yet the bright, thickly painted

Jamaican colors of blue, red, and green celebrate the pride of the structure's youthful creator. I still have in my journal the picture of Jermaine and his wife, with a toddler in her arms, standing in front of the beach shack. The baby was sick with a bronchial infection. We were able to take the young child with Jermaine and his wife to the local church just three blocks away, where Steve was running the medical clinic and Mark was seeing dental patients. Jermaine was reluctant to come inside the building at first. It took some encouraging. I could tell that "church" was a foreign entity for him. The baby was treated, and Jermaine and his wife received dental treatment, maybe for the first time in their lives.

We introduced Jermaine and his wife to the local pastor and reminded them that we were not only their business partners but would be serving them through the local church to help meet all of the needs in their lives. Mission evangelism is not dependent on a person's response, nor does it always have to be tied to a verbal presentation of the gospel. Jesus said people would be able to sort out truth from fiction by the demonstration of his followers' love, followers who are willing to sacrificially lay down their rights, conveniences, and lifestyles so that others may live.

Three Biblical Mandates

Jesus' mission centers on three biblical mandates that define the mission operative for the church.

1. THE GREAT REQUIREMENT

> He has shown all you people what is good. And what does the LORD require of you? To act justly and to love mercy and to walk humbly with your God. (Mic 6:8)

We need to look at these actions individually.

Justice. We are called to *do* justice and not just to believe in justice or study justice. You have power with God by your actions toward people, especially the poor and marginalized. Justice is a core biblical theme:

The LORD is known by his acts of justice. (Ps 9:16)

Righteousness and justice are the foundation of your throne.
(Ps 89:14)

Follow justice and justice alone, so that you may live and possess the land the LORD your God is giving you. (Deut 16:20)

The LORD works righteousness
and justice for all the oppressed. (Ps 103:6)

The list goes on! The foundation of God's kingdom is established on justice. Followers of Jesus must always speak and act on behalf of those who lack voice or influence. We must go where Jesus is going, do what Jesus is doing, and be who Jesus is being for the orphan and widow.

Doing this necessitates Christian involvement in the political process. We must be political for the sake of giving voice and vote to those who are denied, but we must repent of our partisanship. Neither the Democratic nor the Republican Party speaks for Jesus and his kingdom. As his followers, we stand in prophetic tension with the systems and ideologies of the world. How then are we to engage politically? It is not enough to just donate money and send aid. Far too many times the church has been guilty of passivity and even participation in the injustices that have robbed people of dignity and destroyed human lives. From the African slave trade to the Nazi Holocaust, the church supported, excused, turned blind eyes, and denied atrocities. When it happened again in Rwanda in the early 1990s (1 million killed in 100 days), we cried with the world, "Never again!" But here it is happening again in a place like Darfur. Followers of Jesus must never stand idly by in the face of injustice but must work tirelessly to do justice.

A group of people from Ginghamsburg participated in the first Rally for Darfur in Washington, D.C., in 2005. We have promoted letter-writing campaigns to government representatives, the United Nations, and foreign embassies. I have participated in two delegations (including members from the Ginghamsburg Board) that have traveled to Darfur. We have met with government officials and rebel leaders. Our people walked in the March for Darfur Rally in Dayton, Ohio, in 2008. Members from our church have spoken at numerous schools, clubs, colleges, universities, fraternities, and sororities to inform and enlist others in the cause. Yes, the people of Jesus must be political in the pursuit of justice but repent from the partisan political alliances that have created dissonance with the message and mission of Jesus.

Mercy. Participants of the missional church will be both activists for justice and living demonstrations of God's mercy. Mercy is closely related to grace—receiving what one doesn't deserve or hasn't earned. Many people in the church fail to understand the critical difference between a moralistic and a gospel worldview. Moralists believe that they work hard to have what they have and to follow God's principles to the best of their understanding. They perceive that in some way they are more deserving or in better standing with God because of their effort. Acceptance of self as well as acceptance of others is tied to this effort. People with a moralistic worldview tend to look down on persons they feel might lack initiative. This is one reason there is so little socioeconomic diversity in the local church. Many of our mainline churches talk about racial and socioeconomic diversity—that is, acceptance of all people—but fail to embody it. A gospel worldview begins with the premise that God accepts me, demonstrated through the redemptive offering of his Son on the cross, in spite of my brokenness and failures. Because of God's mercy and grace, I am accepted and now free to work at being the person God created me to be. Mercy is the generous demonstration of indescribable grace! The missional church is actively and practically demonstrating God's mercy through ministries that provide daily life necessities in the communities where they are located.

As I already mentioned, Ginghamsburg started a community food pantry and gently used clothing store before we even reached one hundred in worship attendance. A Christian twelve-step recovery program soon followed, along with divorce recovery groups for both adults and children. It wasn't long before we had the reputation of being "the recovery church" and "the church that helps people." That's the reputation the church is supposed to have. We were not able to compete with the excellent music programs and facilities of the large churches in our area. It is a bit kind to say that our music was less than average. We had a 103-year-old two-room country church building on a quarter acre of land, and our annual budget was less than $30,000 a year. We are located sixteen miles north of Dayton, Ohio, which has declined in population since my wife and I arrived. But there is one thing any church, regardless of its size and location, can begin to do immediately—show mercy!

Humility. Mission evangelism differs from attraction in the sense that it moves out and serves others regardless of cultural, political, moral, or creedal differences. It serves without expectation of return or self-gain. This is what it means to walk humbly with God. It is not about us or for us. It's about serving Jesus in other people: "For I was hungry and you gave me something to eat..."

In Darfur, the people are primarily Muslims. The sustainable agricultural program we started in 2005 has expanded to feed almost eighty thousand people. We did so expecting nothing in return; we do it because the love of Jesus compels us. In an Islamic country, sharing the gospel overtly through our words can create barriers of resentment and hostility. But humbly demonstrating the gospel through acts of compassion builds trust and opens the door for future dialogue.

2. THE GREAT COMMANDMENT

My command is this: Love each other as I have loved you. Greater love has no one than this: to lay down one's life for one's friends. (John 15:12-13)

The Jesus follower cannot live this mandate and stay in comfortable places. The tremendous work of rehabilitation in the aftermath of Hurricane Katrina is just one example of Jesus followers venturing into uncomfortable places to act in love for people they've never met. Ginghamsburg Church has sent more than fifty teams in the last four years since the devastating catastrophe. Some of our people have given vacation weeks to return four or five times. People spend Thanksgiving and Christmas breaks lifting the hopes and restoring the residences of those who have been ripped off by insurance companies and contractors.

Can you imagine how the world would be different if the church went out of business today? Think of all the economies and social services that would be affected due to the lost unpaid servant labor and financial resources: schools, clinics, day cares, counseling centers, intervention and faith-based programs, homeless shelters, food pantries, GED programs, senior programs— Need I go on? The church is the largest nongovernment/nonprofit social agency in the United States. Would your community be different if your church closed its doors tomorrow?

3. THE GREAT COMMISSION

> All authority in heaven and earth has been given to me. Therefore go and make disciples of all nations, baptizing them in the name of the Father and of the Son and of the Holy Spirit, and teaching them to obey everything I have commanded you. (Matt 28:18-20)

Mission evangelism serves without expectation, honoring all people as children who are created in the image of God. We work outside the walls, structures, barriers, and limitations of the institution to promote God's justice through the demonstration of generous and practical services of mercy. We promote Christlike lifestyles of sacrifice and simplicity that demonstrate the love of God revealed in the cross. Yet this is all to no avail if we are not actively committed to building authentic Christ follower-disciples. We will deal with this more thoroughly in chapter 3.

Right Religion

David Kinnaman and Gabe Lyons's research in *Unchristian: What a New Generation Really Thinks about Christianity* gives insight into the absence of a vast number of sixteen- to thirty-five-year-olds from the church. The outsiders' most common reaction to the faith is that Christians no longer represent what Jesus was really about and that Christianity in its current expression is not what it was meant to be. One respondent made this observation: "Christianity has become bloated with blind followers who would rather repeat slogans than actually feel true compassion and care. Christianity has become marketed and streamlined into a juggernaut of fear mongering that has lost its own heart."[4]

My research affirms Kinnaman and Lyons's conclusion that the majority of people who avoid the church are not anti-God or anti-Jesus. Rather, they perceive the church to lack relevance and fail to see how it is making a positive difference in the world. One person from Georgia wrote, "I know what they are against but I don't know what they are for. It seems like the Christians I know are even against being proactive in environmental care."

Many express the perspective that the Christian religion has been reduced to abstract ideas, rituals, rules, and "boring gatherings." Judgment and hypocrisy are the repetitive mantra of the outsider in reference to the church.

It is not acceptable to make doctrine and church meetings a substitute for sacrificial service. The book of James reminds us that the truest expression of worship you can offer God is to serve the poor and live the Jesus ethic: "Religion that God our Father accepts as pure and faultless is this: to look after orphans and widows in their distress and to keep oneself from being polluted by the world" (1:27). Mission evangelism is about practical service to the most vulnerable. In areas of conflict, like the current situation in Darfur, women and children are disproportionately targeted. The missional church is committed to those who lack sufficient support sources. The church that is actively and practically engaging its community at the places of greatest need understands that the gospel is good news for the poor and that God is "a father to the fatherless" (Ps 68:5).

You don't need to have hundreds of people in your church to be actively and faithfully serving Jesus' mission. The people of Bald Knob UMC are doing it with fewer than fifteen! Where do you see a great need in your community or the world? Quit worrying about getting people into your church, and start finding opportunities to move the people who are already there out into God's service. Religion that honors God is religion with feet.

Questions for Reflection
1. Are there any "cruise ship" programs in your church that need to be diverted into missional ventures?
2. Where does ministry with the poor rank among your church's priorities?
3. Does your church emphasize all three of the biblical mandates—the Great Requirement, the Great Commandment, and the Great Commission—or does one take precedence over the others?

CHAPTER TWO

INCLUSIVE VS. EXCLUSIVE

I like your Christ, I do not like your Christians. Your Christians are so unlike your Christ. —Mohandas Gandhi

Presidential election years can be absolutely bizarre in the life cycles of the local church. People's allegiances are often drawn along partisan political ideologies rather than Christ-infused theology. I have been through a number of these election cycles in my thirty-plus years of ministry at Ginghamsburg Church, but the election of 2008 seemed particularly intense. People's fangs came out. One comment on my blog accused me of being "a leftist liberal" for preaching on the issue of poverty. The person went on to say that "poverty is a Democratic Party issue and has no place in the pulpit!" I am not sure what Bible this person has been reading or where he or she had been during the nonelection years when I was teaching on the biblical mandate of ministry with the poor. How many of you received the libelous e-mails from "Christian friends" stating emphatically that the future president was in fact a Muslim in spite of his personal testimony to his conversion and faith in Christ? Some even went beyond slander to the absurd, calling President Obama the antichrist while citing biblical references.

21

Many of us in the church seek out places of worship that tend to embrace our personal political persuasions, excluding from "true" fellowship anyone with whom we don't see eye to eye. The "Christian" extreme radio pundits of the airwaves proclaim God's anointed and defame the heretical. This spirit of disdain and exclusion prevents many outsiders from experiencing the resurrected Christ and drives some seekers from the church. This response is representative of e-mails that I received while doing research for this book:

> I used to call myself a Christian. Yet over the last 4-5 years, I am leaning toward renouncing my Christianity. Let me tell you why. It all started with the 2004 election and I was disgusted beyond belief by the way the "evangelicals" turned that election into a battle of "family values." I teach at a local university in the engineering department. I work with so many people from so many different cultures, religions, and backgrounds, and many of them I have found to be beautiful people—people that I love with all of my heart and soul and people that I call my family. One of them is a Muslim, yet so many fault me for accepting this person because of his religion. We share the human experience! A person may be gay, Jewish, Muslim, Atheist, etc. I search to know that person by their heart. The more I experience "Christianity" these days the more I want to run far and fast from Christians.

Followers of Jesus are committed to relationships of integrity and truth. But somewhere along the way, we have lost sight of the spirit of the one who embodies truth. Like the Pharisees of Jesus' day, we may know the letter of the law while missing the spirit of God's intent. Given the exclusivity with which many Christians interpret Christ's message, you can begin to understand why there is such indifference and even hostility toward the gospel by those outside the church.

Rediscovering Jesus' Hermeneutic

Hermeneutics is the study of interpretation theory. Some of us of had the opportunity to study this in graduate school (seminary). It did not take me long to realize that there is not just one school of interpretation. There have been innumerable schools of interpretation throughout the centuries, beginning with various rabbinic schools of thought in the centuries prior to Jesus' coming. The Christian church has long been divided in the understanding of biblical interpretation, which partially explains our countless denominations.

In the quest to rediscover and reclaim the biblical interpretation of Jesus, it is important to remember that Jesus' hermeneutic was at odds with the schools of biblical orthodoxy during his earthly ministry. He was considered a blasphemer and violator of the law of Moses. Like many reformers through the centuries, he was branded and ultimately executed for the crime of heresy. Ironically, however, yesterday's heresy often becomes today's orthodoxy. As we follow the Lord of lords, we need to continually seek the wisdom and guidance of his living spirit. He said, "I have much more to say to you, more than you can now bear. But when he, the Spirit of truth, comes, he will guide you into all the truth. He will not speak on his own; he will speak only what he hears, and he will tell you what is yet to come. He will glorify me because it is from me that he will receive what he will make known to you" (John 16:12-14).

Jesus pointed out a critical deficiency in the biblical hermeneutic of religious leaders that continues to plague the church today: "You have let go of the commands of God and are holding on to human traditions" (Mark 7:8). All of us bring to the interpretation of Scripture certain prejudices. We view life through the window of our life experiences, culture of origin, and family value systems. Each of us brings a blend of political ideology, personal prejudice, and folk religion (such as the maxim "God helps them that help themselves," which is a quotation from Ben Franklin, not Scripture) and mixes it in with some scriptural truth to form a personalized system of life doctrines. What we emphatically proclaim as God's absolute law becomes our version of Israel's golden calf. We cannot begin to grasp the eternal wisdom of the written word apart from an ongoing relationship with the Living Word! We must approach the Scripture with the humility of children and not the arrogance of Pharisaical judges.

All Scripture must be interpreted through and in the spirit of Jesus. When you read any passage, you must ask yourself, *How is this like God who is revealed in Jesus?* When I read troublesome passages that portray God telling people to kill every living thing—"men and women, young and old," including children—I can't accept this as God who is revealed in Jesus. Is it inspired? It is inspired in the sense that it is descriptive of a people who are doing their best, and sometimes less, in the pursuit of faith and God's promise. These passages describe a people whose sense of God is still distorted by the tint of their cultural lenses. Many parts of the Bible are descriptive but not meant to be prescriptive (that is, not meant for us to "go and do likewise"). If we view many of the conquest passages of the Old Testament as commands by God to wipe out innocent people, then we have a theology like that of the radical religious terrorists of the world.

God is fully revealed in Jesus. Jesus clarified the moral character of God and the window through which we must do biblical interpretation:

> You have heard that it was said, "Eye for eye, and tooth for tooth." But I tell you, do not resist an evil person. If anyone slaps you on the right cheek, turn to them the other cheek also.... You have heard that it was said, "Love your neighbor and hate your enemy." But I tell you, love your enemies and pray for those who persecute you, that you may be children of your Father in heaven. (Matt 5:38-39, 43-45)

The way of Jesus is a higher way. His followers willfully choose life over condemnation. After the woman was caught in the act of adultery, the teachers of the Law and Pharisees took her to Jesus and demanded that she be given the justice that the law of Moses commanded (see John 8:2-11). How many people has the church stoned through the ages in the name of God, using the letter but not the spirit of the word? How many are we still stoning? Jesus didn't follow the letter of the Law. He fulfilled the spirit of the Law.

Toxic Religion

John 5 tells the story of how, during a Jewish festival, Jesus stopped by Bethesda, a spa that people with disabilities would frequent for the perceived healing properties in the pools of water. Jesus began a conversation with a man who had been experiencing a form of paralysis for thirty-eight years. This man had laid claim to his place alongside the pool but remained in his unchanging state. Jesus asked him the question that precipitates all healing and life change: "Do you want to get well?" (Most folks have the "want to," but far fewer have the "work to"!) Jesus commanded the man to "get up! Pick up your mat and walk." After thirty-eight years, the man got up and did what had seemed impossible—he actually walked!

Then toxic religion entered the picture. The religious leaders grabbed the man and told him that it was against the Law to carry his mat on the Sabbath: "The Bible says you can't do that!" And they were right, according to the prevailing biblical hermeneutic: "Because Jesus was doing these things on the Sabbath, the Jewish leaders began to persecute him.... For this reason they tried all the more to kill him; not only was he breaking the Sabbath, but he was even calling God his own Father, making himself equal with God" (vv. 16, 18).

Rather than celebrate that the man had been healed, the religious leaders rejected the man and his healer for not adhering to the religious code they embraced. They valued rules over people and felt justified in their exclusion.

Have you ever been burned by toxic religion or religious people? *Toxic* means "deadly." It affects our understanding of who God is. Toxic religion causes us to perceive God as being critical, unapproachable, and inaccessible. Most people I know believe in God but really struggle with the idea that God believes in them. Because of the way people in the church have treated them in the past, they are convinced that God has rejected them too. When Adam and Eve blew it in the Garden of Eden, "they hid from the LORD God among the trees of the garden" (Gen 3:8). In the pain of failure we run and hide from God, but God doesn't reject or run away from us!

In the summer of 2000, my wife and I were having dinner with my sister and brother-in-law in Cincinnati. We were eating our salads when Lew, my brother-in-law, looked at me and asked if I was all right. "I don't feel too..." was all I could get out, and then I collapsed into Carolyn's lap. I was in an ambulance on Fountain Square in less than ten minutes. The woman working on me told my wife that my heartbeat was irregular and my blood pressure was 60/40. In a moment I realized how quickly this gift of life passes, but I also realized that I was at peace and did not fear death. A relationship with Jesus will really do that for you! I figured that if I had this peace, it was a good time to share the reason with another. I asked the EMT if she was part of a church. "I don't think that I would be welcomed in church," she said. "I was raised Catholic, but now I've been divorced for two years and am living with my boyfriend." I told her that many churches would welcome both her and her boyfriend and that God loves and misses her. What a shame that toxic believers so warped this woman's understanding of God and Christianity that she sincerely believes no church would accept her.

Because of our toxic understanding of God, we seek life from non-life-giving sources: a clandestine relationship, addictive substances, mindless hours in front of a TV, unhealthy eating. It is not because people don't believe in God but because of the toxins that come from God's people. Our attitudes that stem from faulty biblical interpretation become the barriers that keep people from being made whole in the church. Jesus referred to these toxins as the yeast of the Pharisees. The *gospel* means "good news." But for so many people their perception of the gospel is not good news but a gospel of "you can't do that!" The Pharisees had a biblical hermeneutic that focused on rigid rules and rituals of exclusion. Jesus' hermeneutic was centered on an understanding of God who is Life, Love, Grace, and Truth.

An Inclusive God

"Our Father who art..." These words contain possibly the most revolutionary understanding about God that Jesus brought into the world. God is our Father! God is not exclusive to one tribe or nation, but God is Father of all nations, tribes, and peoples on the earth. It is significant that on the day of Pentecost (the birthday of the church), the spirit of God was not given until God-fearing people were gathered from "every nation under heaven" (see Acts 2). The list is truly amazing in its inclusivity. God was even inclusive in language. Everyone present heard the word in his or her native tongue. None was left out. The first Christians were Jews. And guess what? Arabs were also invited to the party. Even the Cretans are mentioned, and they were at the top of everyone's list of folks you never want to date your children or to move in next door! God truly wants us to be one big, happy family.

I must admit that it is sometimes difficult for me to experience God as my loving Father who accepts me and created me uniquely with a plan and a purpose. What happens when you find yourself coming up over a rise on the highway and you see a police officer on the side of the road ahead? You immediately hit the brakes. It doesn't even matter if you were traveling five miles under the speed limit. Your palms sweat, and there is an increase in heart rate. You can't help it. The response is subconscious and involuntary. There are a lot of places where I want to see armed police, including on our church campuses for special events. But never when I am traveling down the highway. It is the same in our encounters and experiences with God. You don't want to run into a cosmic cop when you're heading down life's highway. Guilt creates subconscious avoidance. A loving, all-powerful parent is an altogether different matter. We have all experienced to some degree the toxins of Pharisaical teaching that portrays God more as a condemning judge than as a loving parent who doesn't condemn but disciplines us in our failures for future health and success.

If you are a parent, you can understand to some small degree the love and acceptance that God feels toward us. I am a father and grandfather, and I have definitely found that precarious economic times can have the positive effect of creating tighter family bonds and commitments. Even as empty nesters, Carolyn and I are committed to using whatever resources at our disposal to further the well-being of our children. Our son, Jonathan, is in his last years of medical school. Carolyn and I made sure that both of our children got through their undergrad programs without debt, but we've agreed that they pay for their graduate work. It is called growing up! As the economy grows more dismal, however, student loans are becoming scarce. "What happens if Jonathan's medical school loan is canceled?" Carolyn asked, looking over the newspaper at breakfast one morning. As Dad, I had already thought through a plan for provision and didn't have to wait to provide a response. "Even if we had to take a significant loss on the sale, we still have enough equity in our house that would cover the rest of his schooling," I said. "We could live in an apartment." Now if I am willing to make this kind of sacrifice as an imperfect father, then "how much more will your Father in heaven give good gifts to those who ask him!" (Matt 7:11).

I can't think of any failure so great that it would cause me to banish my children from my life or home. They could choose on their own to walk away from my love and provision, but I would not give up on or forsake them in their failure. Jesus communicated the truth of the all-inclusive love of the Father through simple stories rather than complex theological commentaries on following rules: "There was a man who had two sons. The younger one said to his father, 'Father give me my share of the estate'" (Luke 15:11-12). Isn't this just like all of us at times? We want God's protection and provision while we "do life" on our own. When we finally come to our senses and realize that we have been living like pigs and with pigs, we find not a condemning judge but a father who throws a welcome-home bash! While the son "was still a long way off, his father saw him and was filled with compassion for him; he ran to his son, threw his arms around him and kissed him" (15:20). God never runs or hides from us in our brokenness; he runs to us.

If God is the God of love, then how can the church be unloving, mean-spirited, internally focused, and exclusive? Since I passed the age of fifty, I have discovered that periodic tests are required for cancer screening. However, one cancer goes easily undetected and requires regular self-exams: the cancer of a judgmental spirit. As I stated in the first part of this chapter, in

U.S. election years this cancerous spirit comes out of remission. These judgmental demons of divisiveness have no place among God's people. In places like Belfast, Ireland, Christians fight and even kill other Christians. We divide ourselves over doctrinal differences. One local Christian college will not let the faculty or staff participate at Ginghamsburg Church because of our doctrinal differences on baptism. We live in a post-Christian world that readily identifies the disconnect between our message and life practice, and we can't even get along with one another!

The Apostle Peter faced his own demons of judgment and exclusion when leading the church in the days after Pentecost. He finally caught the vision for God's inclusive kingdom, but it took a while. It is truly amazing how hard it can be to overcome cultural religious prejudices like the kosher food laws that Peter embraced. Peter even tried to argue his theological position with God: "Surely not, Lord! . . . I have never eaten anything impure or unclean" (Acts 10:14). "The voice spoke to him a second time, 'Do not call anything impure that God has made clean'" (v. 15). Peter's worldview began to shift from seeing God as a God of exclusion to a God of inclusion. Peter's next action was off-the-charts radical for a first-century Palestinian Jew! He dined in the home of a Gentile. "You are well aware that it is against our law for a Jew to associate with Gentiles or visit them. But God has shown me that I should not call anyone impure or unclean," Peter told his host. "I now realize how true it is that God does not show favoritism but accepts those from every nation who fear him and do what is right. You know the message God sent the people of Israel, announcing the good news of peace through Jesus Christ, who is Lord of all" (vv. 27, 34-36). As Peter finally realized, the kingdom of God is an inclusive, externally focused, global mission movement driven by God's redeeming love.

The Royal Law

The Epistle of James is practical and right to the point: "If you really keep the royal law found in Scripture, 'Love your neighbor as yourself,' you are doing right. But if you show favoritism, you sin and are convicted by the law as lawbreakers" (2:8-9). Since

God is Love, everything for God comes down to the primacy of relationships.

"Okay," you ask, "so who is my neighbor that I am supposed to love as myself?" Great question, and it has been asked before. Jesus told another simple story to demonstrate the most profound reality of loving God and neighbor. The parable of the Good Samaritan is the antithesis to the theologically correct version of religious righteousness (Luke 10:25-37). A man who had been on a business trip was beaten by robbers and left along the side of the road for dead. As happens so many times in our world, people continued to drive past the man, unwilling to get involved for a variety of reasons. And it was the religious folk who rolled on past without stopping! The church continues to drive by the Darfurs of this world if for no other reason than we churchgoers don't know what to do. But Jesus' story took a pointed turn: "A Samaritan, as he traveled, came where the man was; and when he saw him, he took pity on him" (v. 33). For the religious Jew, the phrase "good Samaritan" would have been an oxymoron. The Samaritans were the mixed-race peoples who were the descendants of the Babylonian captors and the Jewish remnant that had not been deported during the captivity in the sixth century B.C. Samaria was located between Judea in the south and Galilee in the north. The Samaritans were considered "unclean" because of their mixed heritage. A righteous Jewish person traveling from the north or south would add several days to the journey by traveling around Samaria in order to avoid contact with "unrighteousness." That was not the practice of Jesus, however, as demonstrated through his encounter with the Samaritan woman at the well. The Samaritans rejected much of Jewish religion, including the means of atonement and the place of sacrifice, which for the Jews was centered in the temple at Jerusalem. Yet Jesus used this unrighteous Samaritan with an errant biblical hermeneutic as the illustration of righteousness: "'Which of these three do you think was a neighbor to the man who fell into the hands of robbers?' The expert in the law replied, 'The one who had mercy on him.' Jesus told him, 'Go and do likewise'" (vv. 36-37). Point made: right action trumps right doctrine when all is said and done! Does truth matter? Absolutely, but

God's truth will always be demonstrated through loving, redemptive actions. The fruit is the revealing proof of the root.

James's phrase—"the royal law found in Scripture"—refers to the law of the King, or the law belonging to the King. The religious Jew in the first century was committed to the keeping of more than six hundred commandments. Jesus summarized all these duties in one: "A new command I give you: Love one another. As I have loved you, so you must love one another. By this everyone will know that you are my disciples, if you love one another" (John 13:34-35). The love of God is not an emotion but a choice. God has created us as relational beings. We are made to live in trusting relationships of health and fidelity with God and one another. God designed the union of marriage so that we can experience commitment to a monotheistic God, whom we can't see, by choosing to faithfully serve and support another human being in monogamous trust. We love and serve God as we love and serve each other. Some days I don't feel like being married, but it doesn't matter what I feel. That's why the vow that we make on our wedding day is not "do you love?" but "will you love?" Will you choose to love and support each other for life whether you feel like it or not?

The volitional commitment to Jesus as Lord and ultimate authority mandates the church to step out by faith and take action in places of great pain and need. James wrote, "Faith by itself, if it is not accompanied by action, is dead [stillborn]" (2:17). What does it mean to be Christ's body in the world? We as the church are the only hands that Jesus has to rebuild in broken places. Our feet are his only feet to march in the war against poverty and injustice. Our voices are his voice to share the good news of eternal life and offer hope to the hopeless. Our bank accounts are the only fiscal resources he has to carry out the Father's mission. Sisters and brothers, if we don't take action, who will? And if we don't act now, then when?

Now is not the time, church, to hunker down in the bunkers of our sanctuaries and fellowship halls to wait out this economic tsunami. Today is the day of salvation! Today is the day of the Lord! Now is the time for the people of God to arise! Now is the time for the church to be the church! Why must we step out and risk in this time of great economic uncertainty? Not because we will have fun (there will be some out-of-sight adventure along the way, however), not because the mission will lack risk or loss, not because it will reverse our financial situations, and not because it will make us happy. We must go because that is where Jesus is going. We must go because Jesus calls us to go with him. We must go because it is the will of the Father! Discipleship is based in our devotion to Jesus Christ. Jesus' first allegiance was to the will of the Father, and so it must be ours.

God of Grace

My parents sent me to kindergarten when I was just a few days past my fifth birthday. I was always among the youngest in my class, trailing behind in both maturity and physical coordination. I had the attention span of the family's Irish setter. My fourth grade teacher failed me, but the principal overrode that decision and I was passed to the fifth grade. This was my first memorable experience of grace (receiving what I had not deserved or earned). My life would look much different than it does today if it wasn't for that gift of grace from Principal Caldwell. I never would have met my wife the year she came home from college to student teach while I was working with the church youth group. My children and grandchild would not be here. Both of my kids are active Christians and work in the medical field. Our daughter, Kristen, works in the neonatal unit at Children's Hospital in Boston. Our son, Jonathan, is preparing for a residency in trauma surgery at Wright State University. What would have become of all the lives they will touch? My bishop would not have sent me to Ginghamsburg Church in 1979 because I would have been one year behind, and that little congregation might have died out rather than become a catalyst for mission to God's people worldwide. How different the world would be if Principal Caldwell had not made that one, small, gracious decision.

Like Principal Caldwell, God is the God of another chance. Look at God's list of "who's who" in the Bible. Most folks are not there because they were heroic and did the right thing. They were screwups! Moses had an anger management problem that resulted in manslaughter. David had a sexual obsession that led to the order of a Mafioso-style hit on one of his officers. The Bible is not a book about righteous people who serve as heroic examples; it is about a gracious God who uses us in spite of our brokenness and never lets go until we become who God created us to be.

The long lists of genealogies in the Bible seem inconsequential and easy to skip over. There is one in Matthew's list, however, that reveals the scope of God's outrageous grace. Perez, the son of Judah and Judah's daughter-in-law, Tamar, was conceived in the arms of deception and distorted passion that would make the scenarios of *Desperate Housewives* seem tame (you can read the details in Gen 38). Talk about grace; these screwed-up people were chosen to be in the DNA line of the Messiah!

I admit it can be hard to live in the paradox of grace and truth. One of the biggest issues of inclusion that the church faces today is the issue of homosexuality. The controversy is not going to go away, and the church needs to be involved in healing and loving ways with our sons and daughters, friends and neighbors, mothers and fathers who are gay and lesbian. As a pastor, I have not found this to be an easy issue to resolve within myself. I cannot dismiss biblical instruction, nor can I deny the sacrament of grace to those in whom I see the fruit of the Spirit and the heart of Christ. I know lesbian and gay Christians who have been in exclusive relationships and raised children together in the church. One of my son's friends was nurtured in this type of Christian home, and regardless of people's personal views on his mothers' sexuality, he was grateful for the acceptance and inclusion offered to him by his Christian community. Consider what a difference grace has made in this young man's life:

> From an early age, after my parents divorced when I was two, my mother had a girlfriend. From the age of 10 until I moved out to go to college, I was raised by two mothers. Most articles about children growing up without a father in the home discuss how screwed up kids can become . . . but I am a pretty normal and successful 25 year old attending graduate school. My mothers and I lived in an upper-middle-class neighborhood while I was

growing up, surrounded by families very unlike our own. The amazing thing was that although I knew other people were aware of my mother's relationship with her partner, I saw very little if any discrimination. I'm sure my mom's point of view would be a different story, but not a single one of my classmates or friends ever mentioned it as a problem. I was blessed to be around a community that either accepted their relationship, or chose not to discuss it openly. Either way, I feel very grateful that most of the conflict surrounding my mother's sexual orientation was not from the environment around me, but the inner conflict I had . . . constantly praying and asking God whether or not my mom's relationship glorified him.

I am not going to step out of my boundaries and jump into the argument of whether homosexuality is right or wrong. As a believer myself, I have struggled with this topic for many years. It's harder to stand on the "typical Christian's" point of view when the person you're discussing is your own mother. One of the most interesting things my mom said to me when discussing this a few years ago was that she prayed for my heterosexuality . . . she actually prayed to God that I would not be gay. I had to double take to make sure I heard her correctly, but she meant that she did not want me to have to deal with many of the struggles that she had as an openly gay person. I found that very interesting, because it wasn't that she thought her relationship with her partner was wrong, but that she was aware how unaccepted it was by much of the public.

My mother's homosexuality has affected me greatly, but not negatively. I am happily married to a beautiful woman who (while she struggles with the idea of having a gay mother-in-law) will always love her. I imagine Jesus acting the same way . . . regardless of whether he disagreed with the sinners and their actions, the way he brought them to the kingdom was through love. This may sound ridiculous to some, but I learned a lot about how to love another person from my two moms. They have maintained a monogamous relationship for almost 15 years and although there have been many struggles like any relationship, they have stayed together because their relationship is based on love and faith. So, on this topic of gay rights, I think Jesus would have treated homosexuals the same way he treated everyone else, by loving them and sacrificing his body for them. I don't presume to know what the Lord has in store for my mom and her partner, and I will continually pray for God's sovereignty in their relationship and my own.

Where do I stand on this issue at this point in time as a pastor with lesbian and gay people as active participants at Ginghamsburg Church? I am going to let God be the judge and make the final call on this issue. Jesus warned of the deadly danger of self-righteousness. Self-righteousness results in spiritual blindness that makes us oblivious to our own brokenness and magnifies the failures of others. Righteousness is not an earned status. It is the result of God's redemptive work in the cross. When we judge other people, we demean the redemptive work of Jesus and make it our own. Jesus warned of the dangers when broken people try to separate the wheat from the weeds, "because while you are pulling the weeds, you may uproot the wheat with them. Let both grow together until the harvest" (Matt 13:29-30). This is not affirmation for "anything goes" immoral behavior. In our human brokenness we are just not qualified to sort it out.

God of Truth

We have seen how the gospel of good news becomes a gospel of subtraction through the distortion of God's true identity as a redemptive Father to condemning judge. When our experience of God through the church has been one of rigid rules, irrelevant rituals, and judgmental condemnation, there is the danger of going to the opposite extreme. In the attempt to escape the toxicity of rigid conservatism some dive into the quagmire of relativistic liberalism: "You are not the boss of me. I am the boss of me." When we err in this extreme, we end up seeking the god we want rather than the God who is. We create a god that we make in our own image instead of yielding ourselves to God in whose image we have been made. God is a moral God. God has designed the universe with absolute moral boundaries and laws.

I grew up in Cincinnati, Ohio, not far from my grandparents, who lived across the river in northern Kentucky. One of the great formational experiences of my life and faith was spending weekends during the school year and weeks in the summer at their home. My friend Jimmy lived next door. He was a year older and more experienced in the mischievous adventures of the world. On one particular humid Midwestern summer day, Jimmy and I were sitting around talking about the possibility of flying. Not the kind of flying that is assisted by the means of aircraft but flying of the Superman variety. This was during the late 1950s and early 1960s when we witnessed the miraculous transformation of Clark Kent into Superman on the weekly television series that preceded Christopher Reeve's movie versions. Many of us experienced dreams of flying when we were children. We pinned towels to our backs and jumped off our parents' couches with our arms extended. On this occasion Jimmy and I were commenting on the new *Mary Poppins* movie that had just come out. Jimmy knew for a fact that if we took my grandfather's big black umbrella with the cane handle, we could jump off the roof of Mr. Cress's garage and float safely to the ground. I am glad that providence had Jimmy jump first. The umbrella immediately inverted, and Jimmy broke his wrist on the concrete driveway below. I learned something that day. Gravity is an absolute law that is the same for all of us, whether you want it to be or believe to the contrary.

Toxic religion goes to the extremes of focusing on law to the exclusion of grace or grace without the boundaries of absolute truth. But "the Word became flesh and made his dwelling among us. We have seen his glory, the glory of the one and only [Son], who came from the Father, full of *grace* and *truth*" (John 1:14, emphasis added). We must hold grace and truth in balanced tension. There is a difference between being judgmental and having spiritual discernment. Judgment produces anger, criticism, and slander. Judgment is exclusive and gives one a smug sense of satisfaction over another's failure ("I told you so!"). Discernment creates empathetic pain that leads first to compassion and then to intercession. The spirit of discernment connects one to the heart and patience of God, who is not "wanting anyone to perish, but everyone to come to repentance" (2 Pet 3:9).

The toxins of the Pharisees and Sadducees parallel the two extremes of rigid conservatism and relativistic liberalism that can plague the church today. A new generation of young Christians is seeking a way that is neither Right nor Left, red nor blue. These young people are seeking to change the world by discovering and reclaiming the radical and inclusive message and mission of Jesus!

Questions for Reflection

1. How have toxic religion or religious people been a detriment to your faith?
2. What examples of grace and acceptance have you experienced in your life?
3. In what ways can the church better practice God's gracious inclusivity?

CHAPTER THREE

DISCIPLES vs. DECISIONS

The quality of the church's leadership is directly proportional to the quality of discipleship. If we fail in the area of making disciples, we should not be surprised if we fail in the area of leadership development. —Alan Hirsch

The Christian church in its embryonic state was an unofficial movement that existed in tension with the established religious institution and the Roman state. This "new cult" lacked the institutional structures, such as a credentialed priesthood and buildings, which would give it the validation of an official religion. It was driven by a passionate belief that a revolutionary leader had come to establish a countercultural kingdom on earth. The early followers of this movement believed that the way of this Messiah-King was not just one alternative way among many but God's true way. For these first Christians the kingdom of God was not a disembodied heaven after death but a "coming" new way of living on earth. They were committed to being Christ's body of transformation for a hurting, needy world:[1]

> All of the believers were together and had everything in common. They sold property and possessions to give to anyone who had need. Every day they continued to meet together in the

39

temple courts. They broke bread in their homes and ate together with glad and sincere hearts, praising God and enjoying the favor of all the people. And the Lord added to their number daily those who were being saved. (Acts 2:44-47)

Did you notice that last part? People were drawn to this church. They did not see a church that was judgmental or hypocritical. People saw the demonstration of a lifestyle that was other centered and committed to unselfish service. Those who made the commitment to follow the one who could not be defeated by death were willing to follow in his footsteps and pay the ultimate price of sacrifice for the success of God's mission if necessary. The Greek words for martyr (*ieromartyras*) and witness (*martyria*) come from the same root word. The commitment to be a witness could not be separated from the possibility of becoming a martyr. The disciples of radical Islamic extremism derive their identity from the same Greek word. They understand that to be a witness and a martyr are one and the same. But the practice is distorted, and it is based in judgment and destruction. The disciple of Jesus understands that the sacrifice of witness is based in grace and is life-giving.

Without the institutional trappings that are perceived as essential for doing church today, this micromovement grew from as few as 25,000 in A.D. 100 to as many as 20 million Christians just before Constantine recognized the church as "an official institution" around A.D. 310. The church grew from a minute movement to a significant force in the Roman Empire in just two hundred years. Then, almost immediately, the focus shifted from discipleship to membership.

To truly rediscover and recommit to Jesus' first purpose for his church, we must understand the institutional missteps that have brought us to this place. As I mentioned earlier, I am a pupil of the church growth movement. I studied the methodologies and measurements of healthy, growing churches. One of those measurements that all church leaders check continually is attendance. Healthy organisms grow. Living bodies produce new cells. This is true, but attendance can be a deceptive measure. How many people who come to our churches and are involved in our programs are being transformed into disciples? How many of our members live and reflect the values, priorities, and lifestyles of the kingdom? The true measure of your church's effectiveness is the ratio between the number of people attending, the number of people active in discipleship cells, and the number answering the call of God through service.

As Ginghamsburg's attendance numbers passed two thousand, I witnessed an increase in the discipleship gap—the gap between those who are attending and those who are practicing the classic disciplines of the faith, including daily disciplines of scripture reading, prayer, journaling, accountability in a cell group, stewardship, service, and witness. John Wesley instructed the people called Methodist to practice daily "methods" or disciplines. He saw how people could quickly become converted through enthusiastic preaching and just as quickly fall away if they were not committed to daily practices and accountability groups or classes. More and more of the people sitting in the pews were bringing Jesus into their worldview instead of being transformed into his. Now, don't misunderstand me. I believe that the church needs to grow and reach new people. There is a lost world to be saved! However, growth is not the primary measure. Jesus calls us to make disciples—not attendees.

At Ginghamsburg, we take this call very seriously. Only one-fourth of those who participate in weekend worship are members. No one transfers membership from another United Methodist church to Ginghamsburg. Instead, all are required to complete the twelve-week membership curriculum called A Follower's Life.[2] Those who complete the course may choose to be baptized or renew their baptismal vows and interview with a course facilitator to ensure they commit to regular worship attendance, a cell community for accountability and growth, a place of service, and the biblical tithe. In other words, members commit to grow as disciples—not remain attendees.

The Priesthood of All Believers

A recurring mistake throughout the life cycles of the church is our reliance on a "professional" model of ministry. Even Jesus didn't possess the pedigree for the official priesthood. He was from the tribe of Judah, and only those from the tribe of Levi could be priests. The Christian movement began without a professionally credentialed priesthood. Every follower was anointed and appointed by the Spirit to use the gifts that he or she was given for the benefit of Christ's body and mission. Other members of the body demonstrated and affirmed these gifts. Every member was a minister. If you belonged to Christ, then you were a functioning member of his body. Just like the members of your physical body, every member has a function. Your hand can't work apart from your wrist, which can't work apart from your forearm, which can't work apart from your elbow. I think you get the picture.

As the church became more formalized and institutionalized, a two-tier caste system was created that separated "priest" and "parishioner." (I write about this in detail in my book *Spiritual Entrepreneurs*, chapter 5, "The Priesthood Principle.") We tend to make the same fatal error when the church begins to grow. Growth provides the fiscal resources to increase professional staff and programming. The experience of mission that was once the task of an unpaid servant is now assigned to a paid staff person. Unpaid servants are assigned the passive work of committees while paid staff performs the active role of mission. The unintended consequence is the shift from the experiential model, where one learns by doing, to the academy model, where one learns through study. Discipleship occurs in the active process of doing. We err when we try to create transformation in people's lives through the transference of concepts rather than through participation in mission. The disciples learned as they traveled and ministered with Jesus. We fail to make disciples when we reduce the meaning of discipleship to the assimilation of ideas.

When Ginghamsburg Church had fewer than one hundred people, I was the only salaried staff person. Every hand was needed to accomplish the aggressive mission agenda that we were called to do. Peggy began the gently used clothing store; Sue, the food pantry. A local school teacher/track coach created one of the most mission-driven student ministry programs in the country. Two years later Mike became our second full-time staff person. Mary oversaw the newly formed cell group ministry, and Lou created a children's program and, within five years, a preschool day care.

Dean directed our visitation and hospital teams, and Tom organized our mission teams. Randy put together four worship teams, and Rose led the prayer chain. Diane and Len nurtured seekers through the membership assimilation process. The church of fewer than one hundred people had fifty to sixty disciples functioning as unpaid staff with a budget of $27,000 a year.

In the first chapter, we discussed the Great Commission as one of the three mission mandates that become the measures of effectiveness for the church. In a postresurrection appearance, Jesus gave this directive to his disciples: "All authority in heaven and on earth has been given to me. Therefore go and make disciples of all nations, baptizing them in the name of the Father and of the Son and of the Holy Spirit, and teaching them to obey everything I have commanded you. And surely I am with you always, to the very end of the age" (Matt 28:18-20). Disciple making is the business of the church! It is easy to forget our commission and to substitute church building for disciple building. We become absorbed in building programs, budgets, staffs, and facilities—and have I mentioned attendance? We can spend a whole lifetime in the construction of a ministry that has nothing to do with Christ's commission, despite giving the appearance of success. Don't get distracted in building the church instead of disciples. It can easily become a distraction in challenging economic times. Jesus said, "I will build my church, and the gates of death will not overcome it" (Matt 16:18). Church building is his job. Then what's ours? "Go and make disciples!"

Disciples model the message. They replicate the life and mission of Jesus in the world. When Peter and John met the lame beggar at the temple, they demonstrated the presence of God's power and authority in the man's healing. A disciple's commitment, authority, and experience in mission go way beyond throwing a coin in the offering plate. A disciple has spiritual authority. Mother Teresa said, "We must become holy not because we want to feel holy but because Christ must be able to live his life fully in us."[3] Disciples operate out of a sense of calling that is spiritually motivated. Disciples do not need to be coerced. Their commitment is active and spiritually sustained. Like the prophets and saints who have gone before them, disciples have heard the voice of God asking: "Whom shall I send? And who will go for us?" They have willingly responded: "Here am I. Send me!" (Isa 6:8).

The first task of disciple making is an awakening process. We assist the initiate in identifying God's unique mission for his or her life.

A friend of mine gave me a Garmin GPS navigational device for my car. The technology is amazing! A very human-sounding computerized voice directs me throughout the duration of my trip. I can choose the language and accent. The voice tells me when I have made a wrong turn and recalculates directions to get me back on course. As "smart" as this device is, an essential factor is needed for it to work: I must enter the destination before I begin the journey. It is the same with our life mission. We must know the destination to fulfill our life destiny. God has created each of us with a purpose. David wrote in Psalm 139:

> You created my inmost being;
> you knit me together in my mother's womb....
> All the days ordained for me
> were written in your book
> before one of them came to be. (vv. 13, 16)

Understanding your life purpose is discovering why you are alive and knowing the contribution that you want to leave behind.

Some people confuse life purpose with goals. When I ask young students about their life purpose, they will often recite a list of goals instead: "I want to go to college, then find a great job, get married...raise a family...pay off college loans...make a lot of money." Goals are worthless unless you have a defining life mission that brings all of your goals together. Life purpose is not to be confused with a job. You can lose your job, but you can't lose your life mission. Moses had two careers during his first eighty years. For the first forty he was a prince of Egypt. Pretty impressive career! His next forty years were given to the management of his father-in-law's business. Then at eighty years of age, Moses had his burning bush moment and discovered his life purpose. This is the first work of discipleship, Church. We are to assist people in the discovery of their burning bush and then throw gasoline on their life passion!

DISCIPLESHIP TRAINING TOOL #1: L.I.F.E. ABUNDANT

When people on the path of discipleship ask, "How can I discover my life purpose?" I share this acronym that can be used as a simple tool. Jesus came that we may have L.I.F.E abundant!

Love. *What do you love? I don't mean in the casual sense like "I love chocolate chip ice cream." What are you truly passionate about? What rings the bell deep within your soul? Søren Kirkegaard said that understanding what God wants you to do is about finding the idea for which you can live or die. Dr. Martin Luther King, Jr. spoke of the passion that drove his life mission in his last sermon the evening before his assassination, that he would like to live a long life but must do the will of God. Just forty years after Dr. King's death, an African American assumed the most powerful public office in the world. God speaks through the deep passions that we have in the recesses of our lives.*

Influences. *Who are the key influencers and influences in your life that have helped shape your understanding of who and whose you are? I needed to fulfill a history requirement my sophomore year at the University of Cincinnati, so I took a course called American Issues and Problems. The class dealt with many issues that our country continues to struggle with today—poverty, race relations, the environment, and so on. This class rang my bell! I transferred to the school of social work my junior year, and the passion of Professor Hartmann's class has been a significant influence in shaping my life mission.*

Faith. *Faith is what you have at your center—the core reality, the core truth that becomes the determining factor in all of your life priorities and decisions. Your core life belief becomes the hub that aligns all of the spokes (daily commitments, priorities, relationships, investments) that turn the wheel of your life. It comes down to the hub that is holding all of the priorities and activities of your life in place. Who or what is currently the hub of your core life truth? You cannot understand your own meaning until you see yourself as part of something much greater than*

> *yourself. Dependence on God's presence and promise of provision is the key for a successful life mission.*
>
> Experience. *The place where you are standing right now is holy ground. You don't need to change your geographic location, church, spouse, or skill set. God uses all of your life experiences, influences, passions, and skills to fulfill his mission in your life. God wants to do something unique in the world through you! What are you really good at? I was always a good storyteller. Telling stories as a young boy kept my behind out of some serious messes. When Jesus redeemed and called me, the gift of story-telling became a miraculous life mission tool.*

Leadership That Makes Disciples

Imprinting is a psychological term used to describe a life stage type of learning. It has been used in describing learning characteristics in animals that imprint on their parents and then learn by following them around. The behavior of the parent is imprinted on or downloaded in the progeny. Konrad Lorenz showed how incubator-hatched geese would imprint on the first suitable moving stimulus they saw between thirteen and sixteen hours after hatching.[4] He used the example of young goslings imprinting on his boots and following his boots wherever he went. Young children seem to go through a similar process, even beginning to recognize the voices of their parents in the womb. We become disciples through the process of imprinting and following.

The church has invested vast sums of resources in programs, facilities, and staffs that have little effect in moving people to the place of discipleship that is demonstrated in contagious lifestyles of sacrificial mission. New converts imprint on the first examples of Christians they experience in our local churches, so you must make sure that people in strategic places of authority and influence in your church (including yourself) are models of dedicated, healthy discipleship. The leaders on our boards, the teachers in our classrooms, the coaches of our cell groups, and the worship leaders all need to be leaders of competence and character. Health replicates health, and disease spreads disease. A person should demonstrate four qualities before being placed in a position of influence.

Engaged. The person must be actively engaged in the life and mission of the local church. The person should be observed in a frontline ministry over a period of time and have demonstrated effectiveness. Remember to measure results and not just activity. I have received countless résumés through the years with long lists telling what a person did (activities), but they are short on the measurable (results).

Inspired. The person needs to be inspired by the vision of the pastor and the mission of the local church. The pastor is the steward of the local church's vision. Vision comes from the leader; it doesn't come from committees. Leaders are vision wombs. The leader must be accountable to a governing group, however. It will only create discord and chaos down the line if the person being considered for a leadership position is not aligned with the direction of the pastor and the governing body of the church. The direction and mission of the church must inspire the person, and the person must also be inspiring. Leaders are leaders because they are contagious. Others readily listen to and follow leaders. If you think you are a leader, just look back over your shoulder. If no one is following, then guess what?

Informed. Discipleship leaders need to understand the nature of the twenty-first-century church and its mission. Before you ever place people in positions of authority and influence, make sure they understand the investment of time and resources involved for training. Every potential board candidate at Ginghamsburg is asked in the interview process if he or she can commit two to three vacation days each year for conferences and planning retreats. We have 100 percent participation at these annual events. All of our ministry teams and ministry leaders make similar commitments to the process of lifelong learning.

Invested. Where people invest their money reveals the true state of their hearts. Leaders must be invested in the kingdom mission. We infect people through our spiritual DNA. Followers will imprint the stewardship habits of the leader. I have not recommended talented, gifted people for positions of influence over the years because they failed in this critical area. The disciple honors Jesus with the firstfruits of the tithe and then sacrificially follows with offerings motivated through love.

A disciple needs a credible source of authority. Twelve-step programs work because everyone who is working the program has a sponsor for support and accountability. People who are working the word and producing its fruit are ones we need to identify and recruit for mentoring-coaching relationships. We are too eager at times to take the willing instead of the qualified. The business of discipleship is too critical to leave to unqualified amateurs.

A group of my friends gave me a week at Fantasy Baseball Camp for my fiftieth birthday. A Fantasy Camp is an expensive opportunity for grown men and women to fulfill the fantasies of childhood. The camp was held at Dodger Town in Vero Beach, Florida. Campers had all of the experiences of the pros during their training camps, complete with the personalized uniforms hanging in the lockers. Campers were assigned to their team of choice. I played for the team of my hometown, the Cincinnati Reds. We played at least two games a day, and by the third day I remained hitless. My coach grabbed me at supper on Wednesday evening and asked me to meet him in the batting cages at 7:30 a.m. sharp. We worked about a half hour on hitting the ball farther out in front of the plate. I went 4 for 6 on Thursday! How did I succeed? I couldn't see what I was doing wrong, and I needed a credible source—a trusted leader—who could and then would work with me to succeed.

Discipleship Training

I have wanted a motorcycle since I was a teenager, but the priorities of pursuing an education, getting married, raising a family, and paying for the children's education tend to delay recreational nonessentials like that. Finally, after saving for almost ten years, I ordered my lava red 2005 Harley-Davidson Road King Custom. Before my new bike was delivered, I took the Honda motorcycle safety course, taught by a retired machinist named Les, who had been riding bikes for more than fifty years.

Over the five nights of the course, Les put us through every conceivable situation that a biker might face. We maneuvered around cones that provided the quick curves and swerves. We practiced emergency stops and experienced the 30-percent traction loss on wet pavement. Mastering the clutch, foot shift, and hand and foot brakes at the same time can prove challenging. Friday night under the lights was test night. You had to demonstrate competency in each of the areas that we had practiced throughout the week. Miss a cone or stop past the line, you lose points. Lose twenty, and you fail the course. Drop the bike, you fail the course. Pass, and you qualify for the motorcycle endorsement on your driver's license. The motorcycle safety course is a strategic and repetitious system of training that produces competence in amateurs who had previously never been on a bike.

Likewise, our training of people in the church must go beyond inducting them as members. We must provide core competencies for lifestyles of servant discipleship. The disciple needs to be rooted in the daily practice of the five classic disciplines of Christian faith:

1. Daily scripture reading. We have developed the Transformation Journal at Ginghamsburg Church to give the student disciple a daily tool to help in this discipline of spiritual formation.[5]
2. Prayer and meditation. Through these, the disciple learns how to listen to the intuitive voice of the Spirit.
3. Life in community. Transformation happens through networks of accountability and encouragement. Cell-discipleship groups are essential in the process of discipleship making. We will talk about this at length in the next chapter.
4. Service. The church is the body of Christ in the world. Every member is needed, and every member must do his or her work for the body to function. In the process of member assimilation we must have an ongoing system to help people identify their gifts and passions to find their unique place of service in Christ's kingdom.
5. Stewardship. You and I are the only bank account that Jesus has to carry out his mission in the world. I get tired of hearing people ask, "How can a loving God let innocent children suffer and starve?" God doesn't; God's people do. A disciple chooses to follow Jesus in living more simply so that others may simply live.

DISCIPLESHIP TRAINING TOOL #2: MOTORCYLE MANTRA

You need to take into account approximately 600 factors while driving an automobile, many of which become second nature. On a motorcycle, however, there are 2,400 factors that a biker needs to take into account, and they better not become second nature. Bikers use the acronym SEE (search, evaluate, execute) as the checklist for all of these risk factors. These same three practices can ensure the faithful navigation and completion of Christ's mission as a disciple.

Search. A biker is always looking at the road about twelve seconds ahead. Where are the cavernous potholes, gravel, or wet leaves that mean little when driving a car but can send a biker over the handlebars? How will you approach the curve? These are all things that the driver of an automobile may not consciously see, but they can mean serious injury or even death for the biker if he or she is not focused on the road ahead. The disciple is always seeking the wisdom of God's word, listening to the intuitive voice of the Spirit, and pursuing the wise counsel of spiritual mentor-coaches to determine how to navigate the road ahead. They seek first God's perspective on everything from money to marriage, understanding the world, and our responsibility to it. You need to know where God wants you to be tomorrow to determine your course of action today. What you do today becomes the fruit of your life tomorrow. Vision is having a clear picture of God's preferred future and then acting on it!

Evaluate. When biking, I want to have a proactive plan of action before I get to the point of challenge in the road ahead. Discipleship is a commitment to self-awareness. Those who participate in a twelve-step recovery program understand the importance of taking a continual moral and spiritual inventory. Disciples need to honestly evaluate their senses of identity, morality, and mission to ensure they are staying true to God's call. Identifying fellow disciples who will offer honest evaluation is also important.

Execute. James reminds us that we are blessed in what we do, not by what we merely hear or intellectually believe: "Do not

> *merely listen to the word, and so deceive yourselves. Do what it says" (1:22). The majority of folk have the "want to" but few have the "work to." Life is not measured in our words; life happens in action. Jesus' invitation to the disciples was not first to believe in him but to follow him. Faith doesn't precede the journey; it grows out of the journey. Disciples have made the commitment to the rigors of the daily journey with Jesus.*

Too many churches have mission, vision, and purpose statements that few members can articulate and are rarely translated into action. A church may have a multitude of programs, but no one is really sure how they connect together for one strategic, overarching purpose. Disciples replicate themselves. Programs don't make disciples. Disciples make disciples. For this to happen, every local church needs to have a strategic and repetitive system of training that is clearly laid out for the initiate. The discipleship strategy must address how, why, and in what a person is expected to be involved.

At Ginghamsburg we articulate a simple strategy for participation at the visitor orientation. We communicate "here is the expectation for every person who seeks to follow Jesus in the path of discipleship at Ginghamsburg." The strategic practice needs to move people in their development to love God, love people, and serve the world.

To accomplish this, we ask people to live in the life rhythm of celebration, cell, and call.

Celebration. We learn to love God as we worship together in community and experience the teaching of God's word and sacrament. Participation in weekly public worship and daily personal worship is essential to the process of transformation.

Cell. We learn to love one another as we meet together in cell community. The life of the body is in the cell! In small, intimate communities, we learn to respect differences and realize that our unity is based not in our ideology but in the redemptive work of God in Christ Jesus. Relationships are crucial to the process of discipleship, but small groups must be about more than fellowship. They must lead these disciples out into the world.

Call. We serve God by serving the world through our individual calls and gift mixes. Doing is the ultimate form of learning. Every member of the body of Christ is called to be a functioning member serving the world in Christ's mission.

The strategy of your church's discipleship process must keep in mind the end goal. Too many churches make the mistake of measuring input, the number of classes or programs being offered, rather than results. Remember, it is not about the number of people who are coming to your church but the number of your people who are actively and effectively serving Christ's mission in your community and the world.

Making the Commitment

In the attempt to be relevant and focus on numerical growth (especially in the decades since World War II) the church has compromised Jesus' call to follow him in the way of sacrificial discipleship. We have called people to membership in an organization but failed to mention discipleship with a cost. The church has asked people to make a decision for Christ instead of make the commitment to follow in the lifestyle and mission of discipleship.

Commitment to Christ is measured not in belief but in action. Most people in our churches believe in God, but they don't trust God. They fear taking the risk of faith to do the work of faith. Jesus put it out there plainly: "Blessed rather are those who hear the word of God and obey it" (Luke 11:28). We are not what we want or say; we are what we do. As Alan Hirsch wrote in his book *The Forgotten Ways,* "I simply do not believe that we can continue to try to think our way into a new way of acting, but rather, we need to act our way into a new way of thinking."[6] Life is determined by our actions.

Jesus' encounter with the rich young entrepreneur provides insight into the commitment that Christ requires of those who would follow him. The young man came to Jesus asking ultimate God questions: "What must I do to inherit eternal life?" He was a seeker, caught between the world of success and the kingdom of significance. Jesus began by listing biblical commandments that are foundational for relationship trust: "You shall not commit adultery, you shall not murder, you shall not steal, you shall not give false testimony, honor your father and mother." All relationships must be based in trust and have healthy, well-defined boundaries. The man enthusiastically declared his commitment to biblical morality but stopped short of commitment to discipleship. Jesus made it clear that the call to discipleship goes beyond moralistic principles to a commitment of lifestyle change: "You still lack one thing. Sell everything you have and give to the poor, and you will have treasure in heaven. Then come, follow me" (Luke 18:18-29). Following Jesus calls for a radical reordering of priorities. Jesus was leading the young entrepreneur through the discipleship process: (1) selling/releasing the world's materialistic value system, (2) prioritizing the needs of the world's poor and oppressed, and (3) following Jesus in the way of sacrificial mission (Luke 18).

Many people in our churches profess Jesus but bring him into their own soft secular-political worldviews instead of being converted into Jesus' worldview of the kingdom of God. The process of discipleship is the focused system of moving people from believers to followers: from donation to sacrifice, from moralistic principles to lifestyles of self-denial, from the pursuit of success to true significance. Disciples learn to drop everything they have into the hands of Jesus to be directed by God's purpose.

Questions for Reflection

1. How many members are in your church? How many disciples are actively ministering?
2. In what area do you need to improve as a leader who makes members into disciples?
3. Does your church have a clearly articulated process of discipleship training?

CHAPTER FOUR

MICRO vs. MACRO

Out of complexity, find simplicity. —Albert Einstein

Carolyn and I lived in Cincinnati our first year of marriage. She had a great job working for the local utility company, and I was finishing my last year at the University of Cincinnati. We had a nice apartment and were enjoying the benefits of her professional income. We moved to Wilmore, Kentucky, after I graduated, and we both pursued graduate degrees, living on my stipend from weekend youth ministry and Carolyn's from her graduate assistantship. We moved into a three-room cinder block duplex that had been built right after WWII in conjunction with the GI bill which allowed many, including our fathers, to receive their degrees. When I say cinder block, I mean there was no insulation or drywall. When it was hot outside, it was an oven inside. In the frozen tundra of January there was frost on the walls on the inside. We had very little money, but Carolyn was masterful at making a $20-a-week grocery budget work in the 1970s. It is amazing how many variations there are on tuna casserole! The floor was 1946 linoleum. We found remnants of orange shag carpeting to cover the floors and painted crates that served as end tables and bookcases orange to match. My grandparents gave us a table that had been in their cellar, and we bought directors' chairs for living room furniture. Despite our shabby abode, Carolyn and I look back at those times as a reminder that full and abundant life consists not of the things we possess but of the relationships in which we invest.

The recent global recession is likewise teaching Americans that bigger isn't necessarily better and less can be more. Americans' pursuit of mega-lifestyles in the last several decades created an unsustainable debt cycle. Americans reached a negative savings rate in 2005, spending $1.22 for every $1.00 earned. We craved houses we could not afford and the latest digital gadgets we didn't need. Bankers were willing to fuel unbridled appetites with subprime interest loans. It didn't matter because we knew we could flip a house in three years and make 25 percent on the investment. We would then purchase a bigger home and repeat the process. Who would have thought that houses would have lost nearly 30 percent of their value by 2009? Our 401(k)s were soaring due to an overvalued stock market. The Dow Jones Industrial Average, which crossed 14,000 in 2007, went below 6,500 in 2009. Struggling American car manufacturers became paralytic when gas prices soared to more than $4.00 a gallon in the summer of 2008. They had failed to heed the economic warning signs and continued to build the mammoth gas guzzlers that the American appetite craved. You could buy a share of General Motors stock at the 1933 price of $1.60 in March 2009, and by June it was no longer listed on the New York Stock Exchange. What had been the number one company in the world at one time was forced to declare bankruptcy.

Now more people are using public transportation. We are driving less and keeping our cars longer. Mortgage-strapped families are finding ways to downsize homes. Layoffs and salary freezes are forcing the majority of us to downsize our lifestyles, and Americans have begun to spend less than they earn once again. The economic malaise has caused people to look for ways to simplify their lives. The economy is forcing people to stay closer to home. Folks are rediscovering state parks as affordable and fun alternatives to expensive theme parks and resorts. "Simplicity" and "getting back to basics" are values that are being reemphasized.

Marketing firms are focusing on these felt-need themes in their advertising campaigns. Their research reveals that people are seeking ways to simplify and reduce clutter, and also to influence the world around them. Eighty-six percent describe themselves as "caring deeply about social injustice," and 84 percent report the desire to "live a simple life."[1] These are the priorities the church should be emphasizing, anyway!

At Ginghamsburg, we offer fellowship meals four days a week on a donation basis. If you have money, donate, and if you don't, don't worry about it. As Jesus followers, we need to own responsibility for the well-being of the whole. We are our sisters' and brothers' keepers! We must find ways as individuals and faith communities to live more simply so that others may simply live. Simplicity means fully embracing and celebrating God's gifts today. In times of uncertainty and crisis it can be easy to postpone today waiting for a better tomorrow.

A Time of Transition

In the 1990s, many of us were talking about the 24/7 church—the church that ran a complex array of programming seven days a week, twenty-four hours a day. The missional church that is engaging its community and world in the places of real need today will not waste time and resources fueling complex organizational structures and programs. Less is more! The focus will be given to the fundamentals of community, discipleship, and mission.

In their book *Simple Church*, Thom Rainer and Eric Geiger have reminded the church of this fundamental biblical model: "Simple churches are growing and vibrant. Churches with a simple process for reaching and maturing people are expanding the Kingdom. Church leaders who have designed a simple biblical process to make disciples are effectively advancing the movement of the gospel." They define a *simple church* "as a congregation designed around a straightforward and strategic process that moves people through the stages of spiritual growth."[2]

The growing, boomer generation churches of the 1980s and 1990s emphasized programs of excellence for every age group. We developed the contemporary worship movement that integrated media, music, and drama framed in elaborate artistic staging. Lighting and sound engineering became areas of expertise needed for even midsize churches. Some of our growing physical plants rivaled small college campuses and our parking lots, shopping malls. With growth came the necessity of leadership and management styles the caliber of those at small-to-midsize corporations. The complexity of staffing, financing, and programming developed over the preceding twenty years left church leaders ill prepared for the economic tsunami. The complex model of the last decades is not mobile or highly reproducible for the vast majority of churches in the post-Christian socioeconomic culture of the twenty-first century.

Churches that had no debt when the economic meltdown of 2008 occurred had much less interruption when it came to the painful decisions of making cuts in church budgets. Ginghamsburg Church had very manageable debt for a ministry of our size that did not impact discipleship and mission in normal times. The worst economic downturn since the Great Depression changed the landscape and rules for future strategies and practices for all of us. Resource management has become even more critical as we continue to be proactive in Jesus' mission of good news to the least and the lost.

Even prior to the current economic collapse, however, other transitions were making the successful church growth models of the last decades irrelevant:

Mobility. Technology was supposed to allow us to get our work done faster so that we would have more time for family and play. In reality we began to work more *and* play less. How many of you get caught up in answering e-mails when you get home from work? I have the intention of only "checking" my e-mails and then end up responding to ASAPs for the next hour and a half. Before I had a Blackberry, I sat in the movie theater with my wife uninterrupted. Now I find myself making strategic mission decisions by e-mail during the previews! Expendable income and expanded debt habits allowed for more play and travel. The generation that was the backbone of lay leadership during the church growth movement of the 1990s is now often out of town on weekends, going up to the mountains or down to the beach, or visiting grandchildren out of state. (I am sitting on the couch next to my six-day-old granddaughter even as I write these words!) Key members have become peripheral supporters. Innovative churches will find ways to minister to these folks through podcasts and live webcasts of worship services. But these strategies will be limited in scope if there is not a strategy to involve the cyber community in networks of discipleship and mission.

Time competition. The DNA of the missional church of the book of Acts is based in day-to-day authentic community. Today, schedules are too crowded for intentional conversation and connection. Younger families are involved with their children in all of the community sports programs. From soccer to swimming, baseball to basketball, the seamless movement from one season to the next keeps the neighborhood car pool in perpetual motion. Sunday mornings are not just for church anymore! And you can even answer e-mails as you cheer your children from the stands. People no longer want the smorgasbord of "cruise ship" activities offered at the megachurch that compete with what the culture already has to offer. Instead, they are seeking the authentic sense of community and meaning that may not be easily recognized in the complex programming model of the megachurch.

Changes in family life. Shared custody and blended families have made weekend time very valuable for moms and dads who aren't with their children every weekend. Those in the thirty-five and under generation are choosing to remain single and getting married later than their boomer counterparts. Many don't relate to the child-centered, family-focused environments and programs that the boomers treasured and mastered.

Networked society. The way that people build relationships and understanding of community has changed. The local geographic community is no longer the center of identity or base for forming relationships. Human life is lived in a complex array of networks, like the social networks on the Internet. If Facebook were a country, based on population it would now be the fifth largest country in the world. People connect through networks of personal interest rather than through the places where they live and work. During my son's baseball years, we were closely connected to a fellowship of baseball parents. From East Coast to West, Maine to

59

Florida, we watched our sons play innumerable games. I have often wondered how this group of Christians, Jews, Unitarians, and people without any faith background could get along better and be closer than many in the same local church. I am also connected to a community of fitness folk who work out together almost daily at a local gym. Some of us are Jesus followers. I can see how groups like these can truly function as the church in a culture craving simplicity.

The Microchurch

While many megachurches continue to thrive, some of the most future-oriented developments in the church are on a much smaller level. Many churches are moving away from the mall-sized facilities that attract masses of people to highly engineered and re-sourced programs of excellence (a macromodel) and toward rela-tional communities meeting in multiple locations with a focus on growing by doing (a micromodel). Although it is easy to get lost in a crowd, transformation happens in communities of accounta-bility and encouragement. Large churches can ensure this with a strong connection between celebration (worship) and cell (small groups), but it requires exponential increase in organizational ac-tivity and resources in gatherings of thousands. The eighteen- to thirty-five-year-old generation in particular is seeking more inti-mate, relational places for connection that also allow for local, en-vironmental, and global contributions of significance, especially as they relate to social justice, poverty, and making a real differ-ence in their local community and world.

Author Donald Miller reflects on the disconnect of many in this age group toward the corporate feel of the large highly pro-grammed church: "I felt like the people were trying to sell me Jesus.... The bulletin read like a brochure for Amway.... They seemed to be parrots for the Republican Party.... They left us thinking that our war was against liberals and homosexuals...it was hard for me to go to church without getting angry." In what kind of church does Miller find himself at home? He has become active in the Imago Dei (Image of God) Community in Portland, Oregon. It started out in his friend Rick's house. "There were only about eight of us, mostly kids, mostly teens just out of high school. I felt like I was at a youth group, honestly. Pretty soon there were twenty or so of us, so we got this little chapel at a college near downtown and started having church." They have moved several times due to space constraints and within five years had about five hundred in attendance. "I love this community so much it is hard to describe," says Miller. "I have never felt such a feeling of family in all my life."[3]

The church used to be the so-called third place of identity and involvement beyond the places where people live and work. It is now often a coffee shop, gym, or other venue where people gather organically. House churches and churches meeting in "the third place" are thriving.

At Ginghamsburg, cell groups and house churches allow for faith communities to develop on a smaller scale. Our cell groups emphasize discussion based around the weekly sermon. This allows for deeper exploration and growth through group participation that gets beyond lecture presentation. The format also gives structure that keeps the group from the distractions that come from extraneous conversations. Ginghamsburg house churches (different from cell groups, which are integrated into our "big church" model) meet together at various times on different days of the week. They linger over a meal together, share a worship liturgy with communion, and watch the weekly message given in "big church" on DVD. They then take time to discuss the message together.

Other groups, centered on common interests, provide a more intimate community even within "big church." Ginghamsburg has a biker club called Broken Chains. The group is really a church within the church for its members. They have their own process for initiation and training, and graduates wear the group "colors" designated by the patch sewn on the back of their jackets. The members are easily recognizable as they sit in worship together in their leathers. The group has its own website. They travel together on weekends and spend a week in mission each year with other motorcyclists. These sisters and brothers were looking for a third place, a network of common interest, not a church.

A Closer Look at House Churches

Ginghamsburg began experimenting with house church starts in 2005. There are several attractive reasons why the twenty-first-century church needs to consider this model.

1. It is biblical. The early church was centered in homes and around meals—the breaking of bread together (Acts 2:42). A new depth of relationships among believers was possible outside the temple courts. The Gospels are filled with stories of Jesus himself accomplishing his mission as he ate, taught, and healed within homes, not inside the temple's walls. George Barna and Frank Viola, in their recent book *Pagan Christianity*, write: "When Christianity was born, it was the only religion on the planet that had no sacred objects, no sacred persons, and no sacred spaces. Although surrounded by Jewish synagogues and pagan temples, the early Christians were the only religious people on earth who did not erect sacred buildings for their worship. The Christian faith was born in homes, out in courtyards, and along roadsides." The earliest discovered Christian meeting place (the Dura-Europos house in modern Syria) was a private home remodeled around A.D. 232 to hold a growing community of faith. Well into the fourth century, Emperor Constantine was the first to order the construction of church buildings as they are known today.[4]

2. It is natural. Simple organisms multiply faster than complex ones.

3. It is highly relational. Nonchurched friends and neighbors might consider it less threatening and be more likely to attend.

4. It is economical. There is no building or staff cost. Our payroll for "big church" at Ginghamsburg in 2009 was $117,000 every two weeks. Our investment in one of our house churches was $3.96 (the cost of two DVDs) for the same two-week period. Cost will become an even greater factor in the changing economic climate of the coming decade.

Since January 2005, Ginghamsburg has invested over $5 million in Darfur, Sudan, for three humanitarian relief projects: sustainable agriculture, child protection and development, and safe water. I visited Darfur in August 2005, June 2007, and November 2009 to check on the projects and bring back an eyewitness account.

The Sudan Project has built 171 schools serving 22,000 students in Darfur. Life skills training centers equip older adolescents and women with marketable trades, and kindergartens not only teach the smallest students but also ensure that they receive at least one meal a day during the hungry season.

ABOVE: A map of Sudan

ABOVE RIGHT: The sustainable agriculture project trains farmers in effective farming techniques for an arid region. Seeds and tools are purchased locally to support the local community.

RIGHT: The worst health crisis in Darfur is the lack of safe water. Often children travel by foot or donkey up to eight miles per day through dangerous territory to obtain water for their families from unsafe sources. In most locations, children and livestock share water from the same open troughs, propagating diarrhea and other life-threatening diseases. Water yards provide safe water sources.

Ginghamsburg sends medical missions and micro-business teams to Port Marie, Jamaica, four to six times a year. Some medical and dental professionals spend up to four weeks annually in free medical clinics providing badly needed preventative care, treatment of disease, vaccinations, and even minor surgeries.

Ginghamsburg's Music Ministry travels to Jamaica once a year, giving talented servants the opportunity to tour local churches, schools, and public areas and share Christ through music. The team also provides "sweat equity" on various construction projects.

Anna's Closet is a "gently used" clothing resale store, popular with bargain hunters seeking quality clothing at very low prices. Our New Path ministry provides free clothing "gift certificates" to families in need, who then "purchase" clothing.

Each year, Ginghamsburg Church's two New Path food pantries feed more than 30,000 people. Additionally, New Path serves local communities through car, furniture, clothing, medical equipment, rent/utility assistance, GED, and pet care ministries.

Each Monday night, New Path hosts a free meal and worship experience called Gateway Café for its food pantry clients. The food, hospitality, and labor are provided by Ginghamsburg cell groups and New Path's unpaid servants. Gateway provides nearly 11,500 meals every year.

Since Hurricane Katrina devastated New Orleans in August of 2005, Ging-hamsburg has sent nearly 60 teams to the Gulf Coast as part of our Extreme Makeover: Neighborhood Edition initiative. Much devastation remains, and 90% of the work currently being completed in the New Orleans area is through faith-based organizations.

One of Ginghamsburg's unique micro-communities is the Broken Chains mo-
torcyclist ministry. The group rides together and travels on a biker mission trip
to the annual "Thunder in the Valley" motorcycle rally in Johnstown, PA. Each
June, a "Blessing of the Bikes" is held to anoint the bikes with oil and to pray for
rider protection during the ride season.

Ginghamsburg house churches provide the biblical model of the church to those
seeking more intimate community and to those who find a traditional church structure uncomfortable. Music, the week's sermon on DVD, a common meal, and communion are part of each weekly gathering.

To minimize brick and maximize mission, Ginghamsburg's worship area serves multiple functions. Each weekend, it sees five worship celebrations (*top photo*). On Monday nights, it hosts food pantry clients for Gateway Café (*middle photo*). On weekdays, the space is used for "music class" and playtime for preschoolers (*bottom photo*).

5. It is missional. A house church holds each person to higher accountability for being Christ's means of grace and healing in the lives of others, including the mission of bringing nonchurched people into the community.

The house church is a much simpler model that is both highly relational and participatory—things younger adults are clearly seeking today. The house church combines the two steps of worship and cell group together. For Ginghamsburg Church, it represents a micromodel that is connected to our macromission.

Our house churches represent less than 1 percent of Ginghamsburg's attendance at this time. So why do I continue with this initiative? Because the call is to go and build disciples, not go and assemble crowds. Crowds are fickle and become quickly bored and distracted. They readily move on to the latest next thing. Disciples commit for the duration.

The Toney house church has been around about one and a half years. Members started meeting originally on Sunday afternoons but currently meet on Wednesday evenings. Beginning at 6:30 with a meal, they move into worship followed by the message on DVD, communion, and prayer. The unique part of this house church is that they follow up everything with a fellowship time after the worship time; conversation, counseling, and general, authentic community building happen then. They have told me that people stay until 10:00 most weeks.

Deb Toney, who co-leads the group with her husband, Walt, shared with me how the group became the healing hand of Jesus in the life of a troubled child: a fifteen-year-old girl was brought to the house church's gathering by her grandparents. She was a few weeks pregnant at the time. She was from a very dysfunctional home and has been through things no child should ever have to go through. She has since accepted Christ and now goes to a cell group of her peers through Ginghamsburg. She has been growing in leaps and bounds, staying in community with the Toneys' house church and with her cell group and sharing her burdens with fellow disciples.

"She blesses our community when we get to share in her

growth and how her life is changing. It promises to be a better life for her baby now that she has a home and community that loves her. She will have an awesome testimony someday," said Deb.

Deb went on to explain the relational process of discipleship that leads group members into service:

> We have had people that serve at house church and then use that as a springboard to step out and serve in other places. Like our adult son Tony, who started serving communion and helping with setting everything up. He then attended lay pastor classes so we would have someone in that capacity to pray with people. He is now serving in his own house church on Mondays with another couple in Ginghamsburg's original 1876 two-room chapel. He is also serving with the youth at a correction facility in Troy, Ohio.

Another house church leader, Bill, has learned firsthand that the house church has the ability to minister to persons going through difficult life experiences in a personal and personalized way that "big church" cannot. His group's experience with "Marilyn" is a good example of what a big difference this kind of small community can make:

> Marilyn is a middle-aged woman who has been part of our house church for three years. When she first joined us, she was going through a divorce. Her husband had been emotionally and verbally abusive. Marilyn was also faced with finding full-time employment as the income from the part-time job she had at the time she joined us was insufficient. Marilyn was talented and trained (professionally) but, at this time, she was also timid and terrified.
>
> The focus of our church was not to try to "fix" Marilyn's temporal problems, although she learned that we would be there for her to help in any way that we could. Instead, our role was to help and encourage Marilyn in her discovery of who God had created her to be and to support, mentor and disciple her into a deeper and more vital relationship with Jesus. Much of this mentoring and discipling took place outside of our weekly "church." In particular, the women in our group spent time with

Marilyn in a variety of settings and venues (lunches, Bible studies, visits to local parks), all of which were directed towards building Marilyn's faith in Jesus. Over time she began to recognize and trust that she could depend on Jesus and in him she could find the strength to face the difficult situations in which life had placed her.

During the next two years, Marilyn finalized her divorce, which required several confrontations with her ex-husband. She also learned of a full-time job opening for which she was professionally qualified. This position was essentially a supervisory position and while Marilyn's first inclination was to shy away from this type of job, her more vital relationship with Jesus and God's word had helped her to better recognize the talents and the strengths that were hers. Marilyn applied for the position, was chosen for it, and has done well in it, even surprising herself somewhat.

In addition to helping Marilyn build a relationship with Jesus, our house church also supported her with prayer, especially during the critical times of divorce proceedings and job interviews.

The Goal: Microgroups Connected through Macromission

Returning to basics—aiming for micro, rather than macro—means reallocating resources so that life transformation and mission are prioritized over expensive and exhausting programming and expansive building projects. We have to ask hard questions about the resources poured into facilities that are used a few hours each week. Our questions must be relentless concerning the programs and meetings that consume thousands of hours of staff and servant time but fail in producing measurable results in discipleship and mission. Often the microgroups bear the most fruit.

Tim McLean owns a small building company and took his first mission trip to Tijuana, Mexico, in 2003. "During that trip I actually felt like I had been in a wrestling match with God and that he had much work that he desired from me," Tim told me.

> I had some really awesome time to discuss these God things with David Phipps and Richard Bender on this trip, which actually led to my leading the Tijuana trip for Ginghamsburg in 2004, which is where our cell group formed. We actually formed our

bond on about the second day of the trip when we ended up at a kind of seedy place for lunch and we realized we shared an affection for hip-hop music, which seems like kind of an unlikely thing for some of us. Strange thing actually, but I really think this was when we all became comfortable with each other and knew we needed to form our cell group.

Tim's group was formed organically through the experience of mission and common interest. They have since traveled together to New York City for the Thanksgiving holiday, preparing Thanksgiving dinner for the homeless at the Bowery mission, setting up prayer stations in the subways where people can bring prayer requests, and conducting a prayer walk around the United Nations building.

In November 2006, the group made its first trip to Haiti with Global Vision Citadelle Ministries (GVCM). As a result of that trip, Tim's group founded M1615 Ministries (Mark 16:15), a nonprofit that is rebuilding in areas affected by the devastating hurricanes in recent years. The organization is currently constructing a training center and school. Local Haitians do all of the work, which is extremely important considering that 80 percent of the people are unemployed. Tim's group employs and trains the people. Tim's calling comes from his expertise and passion. He is a builder who is using the tools that he already held in his hands. Tim finds himself needing to take unpaid time off work to make unexpected trips to Haiti:

> The trip I made by myself in June 2008 was due to Haitian government inspectors visiting GVCM's orphanage in Fedja in which they found several issues that they wanted addressed. I went to do some of the emergency repairs in order that the government would allow extensions before shutting it down. Haiti being Haiti, payoffs are desired, but we try to avoid that if at all possible, hence the reason for my trip.

Tim was also quick to point out that since their cell group was formed in 2004, many of the members have gone on to lead Ginghamsburg mission trips to Tijuana, Czech Republic, China, Mississippi, Chicago, Haiti, and New York City. Tim said, "They make me quite proud, if I'm being honest!" Tim's cell group is faithfully and fruitfully functioning as the church without the trappings of facilities, paid staff, or complex programming (check out www.m1615ministries.org). This micromission is connected to the macromission of Ginghamsburg UMC, the connection of United Methodist churches, and the body of Christ as a whole.

As Tim's group demonstrates, the life of the body is in the cell. The group developed organically. It functions without the typical church trappings of committees, stewardship campaigns, or institutional facilities. Missional movements aren't mandated from the top down but grow from the bottom up. They begin as the grassroots efforts of ordinary people who commit to changing the world together.

Questions for Reflection
1. How have you scaled back or simplified your life recently? Has your church done the same?
2. What microcommunities does your church facilitate, either within the larger "macro" worshiping community or separate from it?
3. How can you provide opportunities for microcommunities to be in mission?

CHAPTER FIVE

MULTIPLICATION VS. EXPANSION

*Normal growth comes by the division of cells, not by the un-
limited expansion of existing cells. The growth of individual cells
beyond a certain point without division is pathological. —Howard
Snyder*

The experience of grandparenthood is still sinking in. Our first
grandchild, Elisabeth "Ellie" Lynne Leavitt, is four weeks old today.
Her picture is on my computer desktop, a regular reminder of a
significant and precious life transition. "Grandfather" (Papa) is a
handle that also reminds me that life continues to move forward
in cycles that are dependent on new generations. It doesn't seem
possible that it has been more than thirty years since our first child
was born. My father was four years younger than I when he became a grandfather. My grandparents were so proud to hold our
new baby daughter. They have been gone almost fifteen years now.
As I look at Ellie's picture on my computer, I wonder if I will still
be here to hold her children. It is all about the cycle of life.

Living organisms progress through the cycle of birth, infancy,
childhood, adolescence, young adulthood, middle age, the senior
years, and ultimately death. Each stage has both strengths and
weaknesses. The reproductive building years can also be the years

of challenged resources. Providing for growing families and children's educations can be overwhelming. The latter senior years may find one with sufficient resources, but aging health challenges limit the fulfillment of long-planned dreams. It does no good to deny the process because all healthy living organisms eventually die. Some people try to fight or deny the aging process. It is one thing to work at maintaining health and physical fitness for life. I have a daily regime for healthy eating and exercise.[1] I want to be involved actively and aggressively in the mission of Jesus for years to come, so I hit the gym and eat right. This is not what I mean by fighting the aging process. People who deny aging and death are like churches whose sole mission is keeping things the way they have always been.

I traveled to Moscow with a group of international church leaders in April 1992 to celebrate Russia's first free Easter after the fall of the Iron Curtain. Mikhail Gorbachev's sweeping reforms had ended the Cold War and allowed for the open exchange of democratic ideas. A large banner proclaiming "Christ has risen" loomed over Red Square. I couldn't help noticing that less than twenty-five yards away stood the mausoleum tomb of Vladimir Lenin, the father of the Soviet Revolution. It struck me as ironic that "Christ has risen" overshadowed the tomb of the Communist leader who had proclaimed the death of God during his lifetime. Christ's tomb was empty, yet Vladimir lay entombed in a granite and marble mausoleum, his body sealed in a glass sarcophagus, cooled to 61 degrees and humidity between 80 and 90 percent. A fifteen-member team goes to extreme measures to make sure that his body is preserved in this state, where it has lain since his death on January 24, 1924. "With current techniques, the body could last many decades, even for 100 years," said Ilya Zbarsky, age ninety, a doctor who worked on the body from 1934 to 1952.[2] Why try to preserve what has already died?

Many of our mainline churches continue to dump vital resources into the corpses of institutional churches that died decades ago. If you are not reaching the lost and freeing the least, you are dead! People age, and so do churches. The megachurches that thrived with the boomers have tended to age with their leaders.

These same churches have also shown decline in recent years. I notice far more gray heads in our congregation as I approach sixty than I did when I was in my midthirties. This is only natural, but if we are not giving birth to new churches, we will become irrelevant to the next generations.

Living things grow. Many in the church growth movement use this fact of nature to justify ever-expanding buildings and programs, but that is not the way nature works. "Normal growth comes by the division of cells, not by the unlimited expansion of existing cells. The growth of individual cells beyond a certain point without division is pathological," says Howard Snyder.[3] My granddaughter, Ellie, started out as a single cell, but she did not pop out of her mother as one big, eight-pound cell! Rather, that single fertilized egg cell divided again and again, reproducing itself in various specialized forms, until there were billions of cells. Likewise, healthy, growing churches will not keep expanding their original churches, but will reproduce new churches. Reproduction is the nature of living organisms, and simple organisms multiply faster than complex ones.

Fish in New Places

The church growth movement tended to focus on expansion growth, breaking through the barriers of 200, 400, 800, and beyond. The model of the New Testament church, on the other hand, was a church-multiplying ministry. The rapid spread of this early movement grew through the multiplication of relatively small congregations. Even though the number of converts rapidly grew to the thousands in many cities, the New Testament often refers to "the church that meets in your/their house"—small, familylike communities meeting in multiple locations.[4]

My friend and mentor Howard Snyder makes the prophetic point:

> Growth comes by the multiplication of congregations of believers, not necessarily by the multiplication of church buildings or institutional structures. If the Church can grow only as fast as buildings are built or pastors are academically trained or

budgets are expanded, then growth is limited to the resources available for these purposes. The early church was strikingly unlimited by such factors. And these are not the real hindrances to church growth today.[5]

The evangelist Luke gave an insightful account of Jesus' call to his first disciples (5:1-11). Jesus was teaching the crowds on the bank of the Sea of Galilee. Two boats were sitting on the water's edge while the owners were cleaning their nets after a long, tiresome night of fruitless labor. Jesus enlisted the fishermen's assistance and used Peter's boat for a better vantage point in addressing the amassing crowds. And "when he had finished speaking, he said to Simon, 'Put out into deep water, and let down the nets for a catch.'" In other words, do something that you haven't yet tried. Take new risks. Act out of the box of your traditional experience. Go to new places. Try new things.

I am not an experienced fisherman by any stretch of the imagination, but I do have a few fish stories. My good friend and Christian brother Bill McGraw has a small place on Lake Erie where he has invited my family to spend time with his on multiple occasions through the years. "Mike, you have to take a couple of days and go walleye fishing with me," he said. So I took him up on his offer. We got up long before daylight, loaded the cooler and all the gear for the day in the boat, and set out in the cutting chill of the early June morning. I couldn't believe how easy it was. I had my first keeper on the second cast. We had our limit by nine o'clock and didn't even need the lunch that we had prepared the evening before. The "Erie Dearie" lures worked just the way the guy at the bait shop told us they would. I could hardly wait to get back to Bill's place the next spring for walleye season. We didn't even pack a lunch. Why was it necessary? We were in hours before lunch the year before. Well, you have probably guessed by this time that our prior experience of success did not serve us very well on this occasion. We repeated the same routine, hit the same spots, and used the same lures, but had only three bites and caught one small perch by noon. We finished the long day with only one walleye between us to show for all our hard work. We docked the boat and discovered from the day's more successful fisher folks that the fish were biting about two miles farther out from where we had been trolling. Lesson learned—you can't keep fishing in the same places.

Bob Roberts is pastor of Northwood Church in Keller, Texas, a congregation with a weekly attendance of more than two thousand. Bob is a prolific church planter with more than one hundred congregations planted out of his church. Pastor Roberts understands the mission of multiplication: "Years ago, I was at a point of growing our church big. I was concerned about how fast we could get there. We relocated, and the church started going to pot; it was doing badly. I was embarrassed; I was humiliated." After much wrestling with God, Bob began to sense a new direction: "All of a sudden this little question came to my mind: When will Jesus be enough for you? So I began to think: What does it mean for Christ to be enough? From this point forward, instead of seeking to be the biggest church in the area, we decided we were going to church the area. That's when we started planting churches."[6] Bob's church plants extend beyond his local community. They are planting churches throughout the world.

Dr. Wayne Cordeiro, senior pastor of New Hope Christian Fellowship in Honolulu, Hawaii, has also demonstrated faithful, effective leadership in mission multiplication. New Hope is a multicampus church with five locations on the island of Oahu. New Hope International has planted churches in the mainland United States, Hawaii, Philippines, Myanmar, Japan, and Australia. Multiplication leaders are paying attention to the number of boats on the water and the number of nets in the water, and to networking with effective partner teams. Those of us in mainline churches have not been as successful as some of our sisters and brothers from other traditions. Our approach has been primarily top down, failing to see that money, land purchases, and programs are not the solution for new church starts. The key lies in partnering with relevant and effective, outward-focused missional churches that are proficient at identifying, inspiring, equipping, and deploying strategic mission leaders.

I am encouraged by the commitment of The United Methodist Church to equip 1,000 clergy and laity to plant 650 new congregations by the end of 2012. The goal of creating "new places for new people" is honorable, but the denomination's ingrained institutional pattern will be to continue to fish in the same old places using the same methodologies as bait. We continue to try to resuscitate small town and rural churches when, according to 2007 statistics, 84 percent of the U.S. population lives in metropolitan areas and 16 percent lives in nonmetropolitan areas.[7] We send our high-potential young leaders to backwater rural places to function as funeral directors while they "pay their dues." If we are going to strategically create new churches to reach new people, we have to take radical actions related to the reallocation of resources. We can't keep putting our resources into underperforming entities. It is going to take a lot more than goals, mission statements, and slogans to convince people to "Rethink Church."[8] People care about the content of the product, not the label. Churches have long majored in mission, vision, and purpose statements, but if right practice does not align with intended purpose, our goal is nothing more than a pipe dream.

Our best resources need to go to the most competent, courageous, contagious leaders. We need to focus our best strategies on new church places where the majority of people live and work. Consider the result when Peter was willing to cast out into new places: "When they had done so, they caught such a large number of fish that their nets began to break. So they signaled their partners in the other boat to come and help them, and they came and filled both boats so full that they began to sink" (vv. 6-7). There is an important analogy here. You can't cast kingdom work from only one venue in your regional lake, and you can't haul the load without a network of supportive partners.

Multiplying Missional DNA

Experience reveals that the most successful new church starts or restarts come from healthy local churches. Institutions preserve the past. Establishments keep trying to prop up the status quo. But healthy living organisms reproduce. Movements always begin from the bottom up—they are never top down. The church, ever striving to reach and serve more people, must meet people where they are and tailor each new community to the people it seeks to serve. Rather than expanding ministries in their current form, creating clones of the parent church, we must birth new communities that multiply the healthy DNA of the parent church while being true to the personality and needs of each local context. Think of this in the same way that you see your children. They share your DNA but are unique in their personalities.

Ginghamsburg is committed to recycling churches and their facilities that are in the last pangs of death. You know the type: a changing neighborhood where the few remaining saints drive in from outside the community, not a child in sight, and no one in attendance from the community. The spirit of the worship on the best Sunday rivals a funeral dirge. We use a "catch and release" model with these churches, mentoring them in missional church practices and encouraging them to go out and transform their local communities.

You can't merge healthy and diseased cells. You can't live with a little cancer. Spiritual chemotherapy needs to be radical. The few remaining people take a vote to become one with Ginghamsburg's missional DNA to be strategically incarnational in the community. The change is radical and immediate. From worship/music styles to programming, all energies and resources are directed to reach and meet the needs of the local community. Every member is a missionary who serves the needs of the least and the lost.

Why not let these fading churches close and encourage their remaining attendees to choose a different church in the same neighborhood? Remember, the goal is to give church restarts a new opportunity to be the faith movement that Christ has called them to be. And you intentionally choose to "reboot" dying churches within neighborhoods where core, debilitating needs are clearly not being met by other churches—because they lack the missional commitment or the necessary resources. From a very practical standpoint, having several easily accessible churches within an urban community is also critical, since residents often depend on bus lines for transportation or travel by foot. You can't assume car ownership in urban neighborhoods.

John Ward is a business owner-entrepreneur who came to Ginghamsburg Church with his family a few months after I arrived and now leads our first wave of restart transition teams into churches that most would identify as dead but not yet buried. John is a layperson with a full-time job. Yet somehow, he is able to begin a process of focusing resistant congregations forward that full-time clergy who preceded him failed to do. At both Medway United Methodist Church and Fort McKinley United Methodist Church, the pastor position had been vacant for some time when John was asked to step in as the temporary pastor until a direction for the church was determined and a full-time pastor was appointed. This process took seven to nine months at each church. Both churches had a history of more than one hundred years, but in recent years their attendance had dropped to thirty or forty on a Sunday. Those in attendance were mostly lifelong attendees who were second and third generation at their churches.

At each church, John asked the congregation to provide a team of four or five people who were respected leaders by virtue of their wisdom and service (not necessarily committee leaders who are sometimes just asked to fill the spot). He also formed a team of four or five people from Ginghamsburg who were seasoned in ministry and wise in the Spirit to serve as a transition team to help guide and encourage those from the church in transition. John led these transition teams and served as the principal preacher on Sundays, but his real role was to teach in every sermon, every meeting, and every personal encounter what a biblical church was intended to be and to keep asking, "What would the church at Medway or Fort McKinley look like if we took the biblical model of the church seriously—really seriously?"

As John says, "It is my belief that there are no 'dead' churches, as some would label them, only ones that have lost their mission and focus. As long as there is one person in their midst that loves the Lord—then there is life. The leader's role is to get them back on mission!"

KEYS TO REVITALIZING A DYING CONGREGATION

- *Start by preaching every Sunday about the purpose of the body of Christ as the biblical understanding of who we should be.*

- *Ask in every meeting: "How is each activity that we are doing here bringing people to a personal devotion to Jesus, not just Jesus' teaching?" It is not just about knowing the word, but doing it.*

- *Ask yourself,* If someone from the neighborhood walked in the back of the church, would this attract him or her to Jesus? *Traditions make us feel warm about our history, but they do nothing for the person who did not grow up within the tradition. Every action and tradition should be questioned, tested, and abandoned if it does not bring the unfamiliar person from the community to Christ—old songs, worship forms, communication styles, vocabulary, dress, activities—everything!*

- *Teach people not only to invite others to worship, but also to invite them to participate in ministry.*

- *Encourage the team members from the sponsoring church to get involved in the partner church's ministry so they reinforce the mission with the church's members.*

- *Ask some disciples from the sponsoring church to worship at the partner church for a while, to help build a critical mass. They also provide support for changes in music and enhance the energy of the worship service. Doing this is essential to demonstrate to the new visitors who would be coming each Sunday that things are different here than their stereotypical perceptions of church. The change in worship styles to one of higher energy and more engaging style is essential.*

Pastoring one of Ginghamsburg's church restarts is Mike Berry. His story demonstrates the New Testament model of catch and release. The Apostle Paul instructed his young protégé, Timothy: "The things you have heard me say in the presence of many witnesses entrust to reliable people who will also be qualified to teach others" (2 Tim 2:2). Mike is a great example of how strategic discipleship can equip each member to be a minister. Mike has never been to seminary. As a matter of fact, he never completed college. Mike came to Ginghamsburg as a last attempt to keep his failing marriage together and is now the pastor at Medway UMC, a restart that is now averaging more than three hundred people on any given weekend. In getting started at Medway, Mike first replicated what he had experienced at Ginghamsburg—removing pews and adding tables and chairs in the sanctuary for community space, opening a food pantry, hosting a bike blessing, and putting on a free festival for the community. But he adapted each of those to make it a fit for the uniqueness of small-town Medway. Mike has also added many new DNA pieces to the mix—including a popcorn machine that sits right outside the main building entrance. You won't find that at Ginghamsburg! Recently, Medway purchased an abandoned drive-in theater. Hundreds of families from the community show up for free movies, free refreshments, and friendly hospitality on summer nights. Eventually, Medway plans a badly needed new building on those grounds but is using the location in the meantime for incredible outreach.

Clearly, the DNA of Christ's mission that Mike was mentored in at Ginghamsburg continues to be replicated in new places. The goal is to church the area—not have the biggest church in the area! You must be a church that is of, for, and about the neighborhood in which you are planted. Having multiple locations is strategic not only in terms of growth but also in terms of economics. A megachurch is made up of people who come from a broad range of local communities. It is not unusual for folks to drive thirty minutes or more several times a week to participate and serve in a wide spectrum of events. The dramatic crude oil price increases that sent the price of gasoline to more than $4.00 a gallon in the summer of 2008 had a direct impact on many churches' attendance. It is more strategic to plant new churches and campuses in multiple areas throughout a region than to expect the region to come to one centralized location.

Changing the City One Neighborhood at a Time

Sometimes multiplying Ginghamsburg's DNA in another location is a vehicle to transforming a community in need. Ginghamsburg's Fort McKinley campus is another church restart into which we are pouring our energy and resources. The Fort McKinley neighborhood lies within the western boundaries of the Dayton city limits. The neighborhood is composed of small homes built in the 1930s and 1940s for young working-class families who labored in a city driven by automobile factories. Many had migrated north from the Appalachian ranges of West Virginia, Kentucky, and Tennessee to share in a piece of the American dream. As families grew and the auto industry thrived, these families began to migrate out with the suburban sprawl. The transition during the civil unrest of the 1960s and 1970s hastened the working-class exodus. The neighborhood transitioned from working-class families who owned their homes to a low-income, racially diverse neighborhood of tenants. Urban flight creates urban blight.

The church growth movement of the 1980s and 1990s did not focus very much on the plight of the urban poor.[9] Instead, many churches chose to focus on the church growth principle of homogeneity, effective because people are naturally drawn to others who are like themselves. This principle works because it is the nature of fallen humanity to seek out the familiar, but it is not the restorative purpose of the kingdom of God. Families who were members at Fort McKinley Church and raised their children there continued to drive back to their church in the neighborhood that they no longer related to. By August of 2007, the congregation had dwindled to thirty or so on any given weekend. There were no children involved, and the average age was well into the sixties. The congregation was all white, using European worship styles in a neighborhood that was primarily African American. The highly transient neighborhood comprises 65 to 70 percent rental properties. Residents do not know their neighbors. Folks fail to pay their rent and move every three to six months. Now this sounds exactly like the place where the church needs to be!

We sent a transition team under the leadership of John Ward in November 2007. The forty members of Fort McKinley UMC unanimously voted to merge with Ginghamsburg in June of 2008. Worship grew to fifty-plus under John's leadership. I asked eighty members from Ginghamsburg to become urban missionaries and make the Fort McKinley campus their place of worship and service. We hit the ground running on Labor Day weekend and were averaging almost three hundred worship attendees by Christmas 2008. In just three months, we had to begin a second worship celebration. And now there were children—eighteen in the third-to fifth-grade class alone!

Ginghamsburg Church is sixteen miles from the low-income neighborhood of Fort McKinley. Our demographic is made up of predominantly white middle-class homeowners. The fifteen-block area around our Fort McKinley campus is 52 percent African American, and the remaining 48 percent are mostly white, of Appalachian heritage. There is currently a 35 percent vacancy rate in this blighted transient neighborhood. There is no way to change our cities without becoming incarnational in the neighborhoods we want to reach. I have struggled to have an economically and racially diverse church for all of my thirty-plus years at Ginghamsburg, and I have made marginal progress. In just six months at Fort McKinley, however, we were approaching a 50/50 mix in racial diversity. What is the difference? At Fort McKinley, we modify any methods, media, and ministry necessary to serve the people indigenous to our new location. We adapt the way our DNA is expressed there to stay true to the character of the community. To accomplish the vision of Ginghamsburg becoming a multicultural community that reflects the kingdom of God, we cast our net in new places, widening our catch while retaining the missional DNA that is core to our calling.

By pouring our energy into the Fort McKinley community, we have been able to meet an enormous number of real, felt needs among struggling people. We are meeting immediate physical needs through food pantries, a grocery co-op, a senior lunch program, and free community meals four days a week. Our gently used clothing and furniture stores and car and medical supply ministries seek to provide urgent care. Some funds are available to help clients with utility bills.

To help community members escape the chains of poverty, we are in a cooperative relationship with the county vocational school and operate a GED (General Equivalency Development) program together. Our goal is to connect our graduates to the local community college. For children, we offer a tutoring program in the elementary school three blocks away, and an after-school club-house tutor/mentor program for at-risk elementary children that meets four afternoons each week. We have adopted Belle Haven Pre K-8 School in the Fort McKinley neighborhood, ensuring that each teacher has a volunteer assistant (which allows for more in-dividual student attention), supporting all of Belle Haven's spe-cial events, such as perfect attendance luncheons, field days, festivals, and art shows—all ways to expand students' horizons and provide for activities that the recession-riddled urban public tax system can't support. Dayton City Schools have consistently been ranked at the bottom of Ohio school districts. Belle Haven stu-dents were scoring in the bottom third among their peers in the Dayton district. In just three years, Belle Haven went from an evaluation of "academic emergency" to "continuous improve-ment." Principal Wyetta M. Hayden swears that it is directly con-nected to our involvement.

We are working with the local township to obtain grants for community development. Think in terms of a fifteen-block, neighborhood-wide Habitat for Humanity–type project. Home ownership creates community pride and stability. It also helps re-duce crime.

Through small business development efforts, we retrain and empower people to transition from the loss of macrocorporations that have closed or moved overseas to the development of self-sustaining microbusinesses.

Social programs like these are centered in the heart of the ho-listic gospel of Jesus Christ. There cannot be personal holiness apart from social holiness, and social holiness cannot be sustained apart from a personal relationship with God. The goal of all of our work is to connect people to the liberating love of Jesus and to empower folks to rise out of the malaise of poverty. We are meeting real spiritual needs through two Sunday morning worship opportunities, Sunday morning classes for all ages that focus on life skills and discipleship, a Sunday evening worship service for people in recovery, and a Tuesday evening Bible study. We have found that breakfast has been a quick way to generate worship attendance at both Medway and Fort McKinley, so there is a free breakfast complete with omelets made to order and pancakes to die for. There is no pressure—or strings attached—to attend. Relationship building between our urban missionaries and neighborhood folk is extremely strategic and beneficial during these meals. Didn't Jesus' disciples recognize the risen Lord when they broke bread together? Through the development of friendships, relevant music, and word, people eventually move from the dining room to the living room of fellowship!

If Ginghamsburg had poured its resources into expanding our current facilities in our main location, we would not have been able to do Christ's work in this other area of our city. By multiplying rather than expanding, we can make disciples who revitalize communities in need. The leadership team at Ginghamsburg Church is currently studying the demographics of other blighted urban neighborhoods in the city, looking at dying churches, and strategically planning our next restart.

One Step at a Time

You might be feeling a bit overwhelmed. True, starting new locations and restarting dying churches take a lot of money, time, and effort. But remember, change is incremental and exponential. Fruitfulness is the consequence of obedient persistence in the same direction for the duration of a lifetime. You don't need to be big or have an abundance of resources. Ginghamsburg began many of these ministries with a total annual church budget of $27,000. We have a Lord who is in the business of multiplying loaves and fish!

The easiest first step in the mission of multiplication is to begin a second Sunday morning worship celebration. It is easier and more cost efficient to maximize space by multiplying worship times than it is to build bigger spaces.

We were able to average three hundred people a weekend in our little two-room country chapel by worshiping three times on Sunday morning by my fourth year at Ginghamsburg. We started a Saturday evening congregation in 1992 and then a recovery church that met later on Saturday evenings in the same space. In 2006, we came full circle and planted a Monday evening house church in the original two-room chapel that the bishop sent me to in 1979.

After you have maximized opportunities with your current facility, look at restarting underutilized or dying churches in neighborhoods you feel called to serve. Reclaiming space can be much less expensive than building a new structure, and dying churches can be revived through the partnership. Several churches have expanded into new communities by negotiating space-sharing arrangements with public schools. Also, evaluate other "third places"—not church buildings—for expansion. I remember in the 1990s teaching in Wiesbaden, Germany, at a church popular with twenty- and thirty-somethings. The church met in a local beer garden that was closed on Sunday mornings. As I taught, I watched my young children run from table to table in the back of the room to grab the stale pretzels and potato chips left over from Saturday night's crowd. In the summer of 2009, we leased from the local township a vacant firehouse located a few blocks from our Fort McKinley campus. Total cost of the lease? One dollar. The township was thrilled to have its vacant building cared for, and the firehouse served as a great home base and launching pad for our student teams serving on week-long mission projects in inner-city Dayton.

Do you see a potential area of need where God might be calling you to start a new venue? Don't be afraid to fail. We have started countless other projects that haven't taken off. The ones that succeed make it all worthwhile!

Questions for Reflection

1. Are there any programs or facilities you are trying to maintain or expand that have outlived their usefulness, requiring more input than they are producing output?

2. What opportunities for growth do you see that might actually require smaller groups meeting at more times and in
   more places?
3. Is your church's DNA worth replicating elsewhere? If not,
   what churches or community organizations in your area
   might you partner with to revitalize your community? If so,
   what churches or neighborhoods is God calling you to
   breathe new life into?

CHAPTER SIX

MISSION VS. MORTAR

That same night the word of the LORD came to Nathan: Go and tell my servant David: Thus says the LORD: Are you the one to build me a house to live in? I have not lived in a house since the day I brought up the people of Israel from Egypt to this day, but I have been moving about in a tent and a tabernacle. —2 Samuel 7:4-6 NRSV

The word *church* is generally understood as a building. "We are looking for a church to get married in," or "it's the church on the corner of Philadelphia and Salem Boulevard." There are no significant references to church buildings for the first two hundred years of the church's existence. The Greek word *ecclesia* (church) refers to a summoned or called-forth group of people. The word was not used exclusively by the Christian church. The *ecclesia* was the principal assembly of the democracy of ancient Athens during its Golden Age (480–404 B.C.E.). These were the representatives who were summoned out from the general population for a political mission. The word as it described the church was referring to the community that Jesus summoned forth to bear witness to the gospel and serve Jesus's mission in the world.

Architecture and space are irrelevant to Christian community and calling. That was why the first Christian communities gathered in homes (Acts 2:46; 5:42). Howard Snyder writes in his excellent work *The Problem of Wineskins*:

> Christians did not begin to build church buildings until about AD 200. This fact suggests that, whatever else church buildings are good for, they are not essential either for numerical growth or spiritual depth. The early church possessed both these qualities, and the church's greatest period of vitality and growth until recent times was during the first two centuries AD. In other words the church grew fastest when it did not have the help— or hindrance—of church buildings.[1]

Capital (building) debt can be a tremendous drain on mission resources even in the best of economic times. Ginghamsburg Church had a very manageable debt (just under $2 million) for a church with our annual budget. Then the economic tsunami hit. General Motors left town, and the unemployment rate shot from 5 to more than 12 percent in just a few months. We cut the 2009 budget by almost $400,000 and laid off or did not fill twelve staff positions. It takes $24,000 each month to service the $1.9 million debt. Can you imagine the multitude of ways that we could be using $24,000 ($288,000 per year) to serve mission instead of brick? I am really glad we did not go ahead with the $24 million sanctuary project that we had planned ten years ago. Ginghamsburg's facilities are rather modest for a congregation of our size. Our average weekly worship attendance is approaching five thousand, but our main multipurpose facility holds only about one thousand folks—packed in. The utility costs in 2009 were $225,000, and maintenance upkeep, another $208,000. Buildings eat money!

There is no question that we are creatively maximizing all of our spaces on the three Ginghamsburg campuses. Most of our spaces are used multiple times with multiple setups each day. Large closets originally intended for storage are sometimes temporarily or even permanently cleaned out to accommodate group meetings and classrooms. A teen cell group uses my office on Wednesday evenings since it is the last space available. I am truly grateful for the buildings that we have built, and there is no question that we could use more space. But in light of the gospel mandate that directs the church to meet the urgent needs of the least and the lost, escalating utility costs, and the global economic crisis, churches must find creative ways to minimize brick and maximize mission.

Theology of Space: Tent or Temple?

Growing churches inevitably face space constraints. With growth come dilemmas to build or not to build, then where to build and what to build. This is when we must honestly wrestle with the issue of theology of space. Buildings define our ministry and values. They also create a certain permanence that tends to become restrictive with demographic and culture shifts. Much of The United Methodist Church's ministry has been limited by the fact that more than 70 percent of our church facilities are located in small towns and rural areas, where only 16 percent of the U.S. population lives. The permanence of our nineteenth- and twentieth-century capital assets has us out of position for twenty-first-century mission. Our brittle wineskins cannot hold new wine! Why are we reluctant to commit to new wineskins? We have assigned sacred value to our physical facilities, and we can't let go. Buildings are not sacred—people are sacred! We need to let go of buildings and invest in the world that God loves and for whom Jesus died.

How many massive cathedrals have been built that consumed centuries of mission resources that stand today only as museums memorializing the relics of the past? The Cologne (Köln) Cathedral is one of the world's largest churches. The cathedral is one of the best-known architectural monuments in Germany and has been described as an exceptional work of human genius. Construction of this Gothic church began in 1248 and took until 1880 to complete. The project lasted more than six hundred years, yet when I visited the church on an August Sunday morning, fewer than fifty people were in attendance.

How many declining churches are using the vast majority of their shrinking resources to maintain a building that represents the ambitious building initiative of another era?

That was why God preferred the mobility of the tent of meeting to the immobility of the temple of Solomon. God imagined and designed the tent, and then King David turned it into a temple. David's ambitious project mirrored the materialistic values of the surrounding pagan cultures. David said, "My son Solomon is young and inexperienced, and the house that is to be built for the LORD must be exceedingly magnificent, famous and glorified throughout all lands; I will therefore make preparation for it." So David "provided materials in great quantity before his death" (1 Chr 22:5 NRSV). Can we speculate that ego might become a factor in many building projects? God gave Moses detailed instructions for the design and setup of the tabernacle, but David developed on his own the temple architectural design that he gave to his son Solomon. God came up with the tent, and David, the temple! The "house to be built" that David heard through the word of the Lord seems to be referring to the messianic house whose "royal throne" will be established "in Israel forever" (see 1 Chr 22:6-10 NRSV).

During the pilgrimage from Egypt to the land of promise, God gave Moses very specific instructions for a tabernacle-tent that would be representative of God's presence with the people in their wilderness journey. The journey metaphor is prevalent throughout both Testaments. Jesus' call to "follow me" is an invitation to journey. He calls us to "go into all the world and make disciples." The church of Jesus mobilizes to the places of need. The tabernacle is a metaphor/model for the church that is mobile, going where Jesus is going, being who Jesus is being, and doing what Jesus is doing in the world. The cloud that covered the tabernacle signified the presence of God's spirit for the purpose of directing the community's progress: "Whenever the cloud lifted from over the tent, then the Israelites would set out; and in the place where the cloud settled down, there the Israelites would camp. At the command of the LORD the Israelites would set out, and at the command of the LORD they would camp" (Num 9:17-18 NRSV). The mobility and flexibility of the tabernacle-tent of meeting are God's strategic metaphor for the church. Inflexible capital assets create systems and structures that necessitate strategies for "bringing the world to the church" rather than the "church going to the world."

Mobility. The mission initiatives recorded in the book of Acts are guidelines for the Spirit's initiatives in our churches today. Timothy, Paul, and Silas "went through the region of Phrygia and Galatia, having been forbidden by the Holy Spirit to speak the word in Asia." They made several other attempts that were blocked by the Spirit, and then late one night Paul had a vision of a man in Macedonia pleading with him, "Come over to Macedonia and help us." The mission team immediately set out for Macedonia, "being convinced that God had called us to proclaim the good news to them" (Acts 16:6-10 NRSV).

Our church board has made three serious attempts to initiate a building program that would complete the master plan developed in 1993. We have traveled to church campuses around the country and enlisted the services of consultants and architects. We have prayed and fasted, done feasibility studies, and spent days in planning retreats. Each time the Spirit has put in our spirits a yield sign saying, "That is not where I am going, but follow me to..."

In 2004 the "follow me to" became Darfur. I had a vision of a child standing and pleading, "Come over to Darfur and help us." The establishment of the Sudan Project (thesudanproject.org) became the latest alternative to a building campaign. Ginghamsburg Church and our partners have invested almost $5 million in the Sudan Project through Christmas 2009. The project is committed to the development of sustainable agriculture, safe water, and children's protection and development programs. If we had followed our own strategic plan and gone ahead with the capital campaign as planned, we would not have had the mobility to respond so rapidly to what the United Nations has deemed the worst humanitarian crisis in the world. Listening to the voice of the Spirit allowed us to move with God in speed and to have significant impact in scope.

In Darfur, innocence is as hard to hold onto as water. Amidst the misery of complicated war, the most unthinkable crimes are committed against the children. Of the 2.5 million people who have fled the violence, more than half are under the age of eighteen. They have little defense against being sexually abused, enslaved, or forced to become soldiers in a fight they don't understand. The world at large has turned a blind eye, as families have been ripped apart, leaving hundreds of thousands of children to fend for themselves and for their brothers and sisters. Ginghamsburg Church determined that indifference was no longer an option. Since 2004, 163 schools have been constructed in south Darfur; 88 of them are located in displaced persons camps. More than 200 new teachers have been trained, and nearly 19,000 enrolled students are being served. Many of these schools are specifically for girls, an almost unheard-of opportunity in a fundamentalist Muslim culture. The schools for boys offer hope for their future as well, keeping them in locations safe from recruitment into armed militias. With safe water yards close by, children in school are far less likely to be victims of physical and emotional violence, no longer facing the danger of traveling alone for hours in order to retrieve water for their families. It is incredibly exciting to witness the results of people's sacrificial commitments.

The children in our kindergarten classes receive one meal a day. It is the only meal they have during the six-month "hungry season" that precedes harvest. Life skills training centers are equipping hundreds of adolescent boys in carpentry, masonry, and other skilled trades, while girls and women are learning food processing, sewing, and handcrafts. On my last visit a woman who had been sewing school uniforms on a foot-pedal sewing machine said to me: "You have opened our eyes by giving us a new skill. We are very thankful." In 2008, a school was opened for 132 children who are deaf at the Ed Daein life skills training center. Many of these children also have other physical challenges, including malformation caused by poliomyelitis. This school is reaching children with unique needs—children who otherwise face an especially grim future.

The Sudan Project is helping maintain the gift of innocence that healthy children require and providing the education and training they need to ensure a future of hope for their families and communities. Ginghamsburg Church has traded our master plan to take hold of the Master's high calling, to give a hand up to the smallest victims of a senseless war. To serve these poor out of our wealth, to live more simply, that these children may simply live.

You may be feeling frustrated that you have had to postpone building or other personal projects due to current economic realities. Have you considered that this might be a yield sign from the Holy Spirit? Did I mention the importance of prayer and fasting in the continual process of checking your strategic priorities against God's? Get ready to move, Church! Get ready to trade your master plan for the Master's. We are a pilgrim people who are called to go where Jesus is going, be who Jesus is being, and to do what Jesus is doing in the world!

Flexibility. Jesus gave his followers a metaphor that is instructive for all of our church structures and mission focuses: "No one puts new wine into old wineskins, for the new wine bursts the old skins, ruining the skins and spilling the wine. New wine must be put into new wineskins" (Luke 5:37-38 TLB). What kind of wineskin-structures will allow the church to be fluid and flexible enough to continually focus resources in what God is doing today?

The Gospels report the story of a woman who had been suffering from internal bleeding for twelve years (Mark 5:25-34). "She had heard about Jesus, and came up behind him in the crowd and touched his cloak, for she said, 'If I but touch his clothes, I will be made well.' Immediately her hemorrhage stopped; and she felt in her body that she was healed of her disease" (vv. 27-29 NRSV). Several implications for the church are found in this account. We know that the health care system was inadequate to meet this woman's needs. This is where the church needs to step up in all the power and with all of the resources of Jesus. We also know that even though Jesus was not expecting the woman's plea for assistance, he was immediately prepared to release healing resources to meet her urgent need.

Some "follow me to's" appear quite suddenly and require financial flexibility to respond promptly. Ginghamsburg Church would not have been ready to respond to the suddenly homeless and hurting in the New Orleans area if we had been committed to higher capital expenditures. Similarly, when the economic markets collapsed in late 2008, we would not have been able to increase outreach by 55 percent to meet the urgent needs of the newly unemployed in the Dayton community.

The United Methodist Church lost approximately eighty thousand members in 2005, but giving in the denomination went up 40 percent that year. What accounts for this? The tsunami of 2004 and Hurricane Katrina in 2005. The outpouring of sacrificial giving was amazing! People want to give their time and money to things that truly matter. Like a mountain stream rushing over boulders toward the valley, money flows toward God's mission and trickles like drops coerced from a rusty pipe for brick and mortar. The commitment to minimize brick and maximize mission has fortified our people's sacrificial resolve in these challenging economic times. If we are going to remain flexible in our ability to respond as the hands and feet of Jesus to urgent local and global needs, our budgets must reflect the mission priority. If our commitments to internal capital projects exceed external mission priorities, we cease to be vessels for God's new wine.

Budget Missionally

A clear vision and prayerful strategic planning must precede the budgeting process. Where is God calling you to go? What is God calling you to do? Vision is a picture of God's preferred future. It addresses the why, what, where, and how. Vision is primarily right-brained and passionate. It evokes emotion. Goal setting and strategy development are the results of vision—they don't precede vision. Vision comes from the leader, not from a committee. A great vision has clarity, a sense of urgency, priority of importance, and scope in size.

We begin the budgeting process each August for the coming year around the strategic priorities that are determined from the vision. A strategic budget will be built around the three areas of mortar, ministry, and mission.

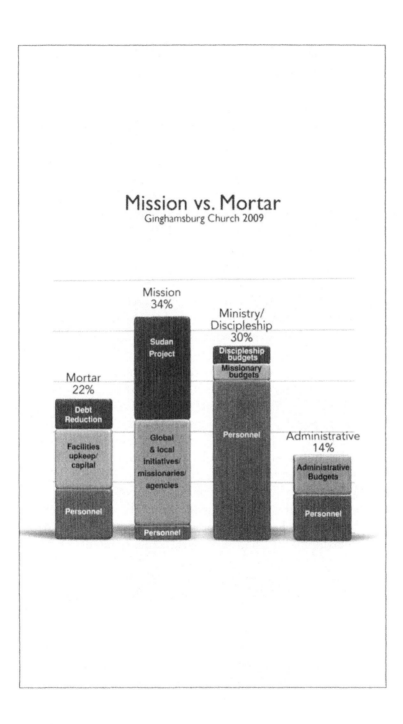

Mission vs. Mortar
Ginghamsburg Church 2009

Mission 34%
- Sudan Project
- Global & local initiatives/ missionaries/ agencies
- Personnel

Ministry/ Discipleship 30%
- Discipleship budgets
- Missionary budgets
- Personnel

Mortar 22%
- Debt Reduction
- Facilities upkeep/ capital
- Personnel

Administrative 14%
- Administrative Budgets
- Personnel

1. Mortar. This section of your budget represents capital expenditures. The line items in this section include all monies allocated for facilities. It includes facilities personnel (maintenance, janitorial, and housekeeping); facilities upkeep (custodial supplies, contractor support, general facility purchases, heating/air systems, equipment and fixtures, landscaping, lawn mowing, parking lot upkeep, snow removal, security of facility, utilities, insurance, and vehicle expense); and facility debt reduction.

2. Ministry. This section of your budget represents discipleship expenditures. Be intentional about making a clear distinction between ministry cost and mission cost. The two areas are strategic in fulfilling the mandate of Jesus to make disciples who will go out into the world to both teach and be everything that Jesus teaches us. However, ministry consists of the resources focused within the walls of your church to disciple missionaries who will minister outside the walls of your church. Ministry expenditures include all children, teen, and adult programming line items and curriculum resources, as well as staff expenditures connected to these areas. All worship line items are also included. The cost of a media person who is assigned to the worship team would be a line item in this section of the budget, though media equipment is a capital expense and would be a line item under mortar.

3. Mission. This section of your budget represents all ministries benefiting those outside the walls of your local church. It includes any denominational contributions or apportionments that your local church might be in covenant to pay, missionary support, staff salaries that are dedicated to external mission, outside initiatives like food pantries, counseling centers, clothing ministries, emergency relief work, community partnerships, and global initiatives. Ginghamsburg's mission budget includes a mission director, a director of New Path Ministries (a 501(c)(3) umbrella for all of our local outreach/assistance ministries), support for staffing at our New Creation

Counseling Center, summer interns to oversee our eight-week urban mission program for teens, our denominational apportionments, mission scholarships, a social work director for our Clubhouse program for at-risk elementary children, support for our church plant in the Czech Republic, missionary support, partnership with a Russian church, and our work in the Sudan. All of the monies for these line items included in the annual budget come from the offering plate. Other mission monies are generated through grants, fees, and partnerships with other outside sources, including the creativity of committed saints who sell items on eBay to raise cash for urgent missions.

The leader of the missional church is committed to make sure that ministry and mission are not sacrificed on the altar of mortar. As a matter of fact, I want to make sure that the mission line items that benefit those outside Ginghamsburg's walls exceed all capital expenses each year. We continue to make this a priority as a leadership team and church board. This means some capital expenses will be put off yet again for another year or more. We continue to delay the purchase of much-needed media equipment while we continue to use duct-taped cameras from 1994. Our total budgeted facility expense in 2009 was $1,105,433, which represented 22 percent of our total budget. The total budgeted "outside the walls" mission expense was $1,685,196, which represented 34 percent of the 2009 budget. The remaining 44 percent of the 2009 budget was focused on "inside the walls" discipleship. It is extremely important to do a budget self-screening that will reveal the mission health of your local church. Use the worksheet on the next pages to categorize all of your budgeted expenditures under the categories of mortar, ministry, mission, and administration. This would be a great exercise to do together with your leadership team or church board. Cast the Jesus vision, and begin to strategize together on ways that you can minimize brick to maximize Christ's mission.

MORTAR

personnel (facilities & grounds) $_____

custodial supplies $_____

maintenance supplies $_____

contractor support $_____

general facility purchases $_____

hvac $_____

equipment & fixtures $_____

landscaping $_____

lawn mowing $_____

parking lot upkeep $_____

snow/ice removal $_____

security of facility $_____

utilities $_____

building insurance $_____

vehicle expenses $_____

capital expenses $_____

TOTAL FACILITY EXPENSE $_____ _____%

ADMINISTRATIVE

Administrative Personnel

finance office personnel $_____

food service personnel $_____

communications/marketing personnel $_____

TOTAL ADMINISTRATIVE
EXPENSES $_____ _____%

MINISTRY
Ministry Personnel

pastors' salaries	$_____
pastors' benefits	$_____
children's ministry personnel	$_____
celebration personnel (music, worship, media)	$_____
youth ministry personnel	$_____
adult discipleship personnel	$_____

Ministry Budgets

management team	$_____
special events	$_____
media ministry	$_____
worship	$_____
music ministry	$_____
children's ministry	$_____
youth ministry	$_____
adult discipleship ministry	$_____
cell group ministry	$_____
hospitality ministry	$_____

TOTAL MINISTRY EXPENSE	$_____	_____%

MISSION

personnel	$_____
general mission trip scholarships	$_____
1. local initiatives	$_____
2. national initiatives	$_____
3. global initiatives	$_____
full-time missionary support	$_____
mission agency support	$_____
special offerings	$_____

TOTAL MISSION EXPENSE	$_____	_____%

1. = tutoring program; food pantry; professional counseling; car, furniture, clothing ministries; free community meals, etc.
2. = natural disaster relief or rebuilding, inner city outreach, etc.
3. = international disaster relief, hunger/medical of other humanitarian aid, development projects, etc.

Multipurpose Spaces

You might have noticed that I often repeat the mantra "minimize brick and maximize mission," but I realize that for the vast majority of churches, it is impossible to eliminate brick if for no other reason than most of us have inherited a physical facility. Multiple models demonstrate simplicity in structure for efficiency in mission. Liquid Church in Morristown, New Jersey, is a great example of a body of believers with a focus outside the walls. They meet in the ballrooms of several hotels and have no plans to acquire a building. Lead Pastor Tim Lucas explains, "We invest in people, not buildings. My people are much more likely to invite their non-Christian friends and co-workers to a location like this rather than a traditional church."

For those of us who have more traditional church facilities, we can repurpose spaces to be more inviting, inclusive, and multiuse. We have intentionally created multipurpose spaces for Ginghamsburg's ministries. Our main worship space is used for five worship celebrations each weekend, a preschool playground five mornings and afternoons each week, dinner and worship space for food pantry clients on Monday evenings, and food court and Bible study on Wednesday evenings. It is also available for local community activities upon request. Spaces that are created for limited use are not practical nor do they honor God in a world where one child dies every four seconds of a hunger-related cause! How can the church justify spending millions of dollars on sanctuaries that might be used for a maximum of six hours a week? Let's reclaim and recommit to the message and mission of Jesus. God is experienced in our service to oppressed and marginalized people. Jesus is served in our mission to the widow and orphan. We cannot continue to build structures that rival five-star resorts and while we call people to follow Jesus in costly, sacrificial discipleship.

Kim Miller is Ginghamsburg's designer of creative spaces.[2] She works extreme makeover miracles on a tight budget. (This is even more amazing when you consider the lead paint and asbestos issues we face in the midcentury facilities of our urban restart campuses.) I asked Kim for her perspective on creating simple, multipurpose environments for worship and fellowship:

Ours is what we often refer to as a "mud 'n' spit theology" out of John chapter nine. Jesus combined a handful of mud and a mouthful of spit as a creative medium for miraculously giving sight to a blind man. Jesus used what he already had to provide what was so desperately needed. With this inspiration, we press hard into the belief that more money isn't always required to transform an everyday event into an engaging experience or to turn an ordinary space into an incredible environment. However, creativity *is* required. Ask yourself:

• What are the colors, textures, styles, and accessories we must use to accomplish the purpose and feel needed for this space (and where might we acquire these pieces for next to nothing!)?
• What resources do we already possess that can inform our direction?

Also essential to space transformation is the unpaid servant makeover team. Teams of everyday people who commit time to carry out these mini-mission makeovers make our space transformation possible. Because the people of Ginghamsburg Church realize the high value of service, we seldom have a problem putting together project teams. Just imagine the wealth of servants in your church who could get excited about serving Jesus with the work of their hands. In the last month alone we've recovered a 30-foot ministry counter with donated laminate, repurposed pulpit and pew wood pieces into wainscoting for a new prayer room, blended old, unused cans of paint into perfect colors for new office walls, and recovered dusty coffee tables out of storage for new use in hallway conversation arrangements. None of these projects required "real" money, yet the results have already blessed many campus guests. Perhaps everything you need you already have!

Kim makes an excellent point about repurposing, recovering, and reusing. Not only is this economically and environmentally sound theology, it is a practical necessity in destabilizing economic times. Look around at the number of urban church facilities that are vastly underutilized. What are the Fort McKinleys of your area? Think of the possibilities those facilities hold to change their cities one neighborhood at a time. All it takes is one healthy mission-focused church that will make the commitment to do a church restart. When we conducted the feasibility study on Fort McKinley UMC before we committed to the merger (do not make the commitment without conducting one), we discovered that it would take $2.4 million to reproduce the same space today. With our mud and spit extreme makeover team, it cost Ginghamsburg less than $100,000 to recycle the facility for effective ministry—and that included taking care of the environmental hazard issues.

Sacrificial Mission

Minimizing bricks and mortar means making sacrifices in the church budget and operations, but maximizing mission also means teaching disciples to make sacrifices in their personal budget and lifestyle, living simply so that others may simply live.

Christmas has become a self-focused orgy of materialistic gluttony for many in the church. The celebration of incarnation offers a great opportunity to bring our priorities in line with Jesus' priorities. Ginghamsburg's "Christmas Is Not Your Birthday" campaign has been a very simple and concrete way to help move people in their Jesus journey from merely making donations to making sacrifices. The challenge: whatever you spend on your family this Christmas, bring an equal amount for our projects in Darfur.

As I mentioned earlier, Dayton, Ohio, has been named in *Forbes* magazine as one of the ten fastest dying cities and one of the emptiest cities in America. In the fifteen blocks surrounding our Fort McKinley campus there are approximately fifty vacant properties. The city that was once known as the Gem City and home of the Wright brothers, the cash register, the electric car starter, the movie projector, and the aluminum can pop-top opener is now languishing. The automobile industry that has long anchored the area's economic base is now fading away. The day before we collected our 2008 Sudan Christmas miracle offering, General Motors closed the last of the five GM plants in the area. Nonetheless, our hardworking, many unemployed blue-collar folk gave $726,000! This demonstrates faithful discipleship through the commitment of sacrificial mission. I challenge you and your church to focus on one area in your community, country, or world where there is great need and make the "Christmas Is Not Your Birthday" commitment. Don't focus on the ones who won't participate or who continue to make the traditional nonsacrificial donation of hanging a pair of mittens on the church mitten tree. It is not about the crowds who murmur and complain. They were the ones who crucified Jesus! It is all about the few who are willing to travel the narrow and less-traveled road.

Exposing our people to sacrificial mission extends beyond financial sacrifice to actual hands-on service with the least and the lost. My friend and prolific church planter Neil Cole says, "If you want to win this world to Christ, you are going to have to sit in the smoking section." Discipleship is an ongoing process of "see" and "do." Potential movements of God will result in stillbirths if we do not move people out of the waiting rooms of our sanctuaries into the delivery rooms of the world to serve human need.

Twenty-first-century churches that have set their sails by the fresh winds of the Spirit are demonstrating three unique missional practices that distinguish them from their classic church growth/seeker-sensitive counterparts.

1. Focus. Primary strategies and resources are not directed toward getting people into church but getting the church into the world. We need to get our people outside the walls of our church buildings so that they can practice acts of compassion. Short-term mission trips can have life-changing impact that forever alters one's worldview and lifestyle.

2. Evangelism. The primary methodology will be demonstration rather than proclamation, serving people in the love and compassion of Jesus without strings attached. Ginghamsburg's work in Darfur is primarily in fundamentalist Islamic communities. We are funding education, agriculture, and safe water programs while trusting the Spirit to open doors for opportunities to share the reason why. I was

sitting under a tree with a group of Muslim sheiks and village elders in the shadows of a new first-through-eighth-grade school facility we had just built in the middle of a rebel stronghold. We had also just completed a vocational school for young men to train in woodworking, brick making, and electrician jobs. Young women are being taught sewing, weaving, and the art of microbusiness (for example, making the uniforms for the 19,000 students enrolled in our 163 schools, bed mats, baskets, and so on). Our nearby water yard will supply the needs of 22,000 people and their livestock. In the respite of the shade on a 122-degree June day, one of the men in the group stood and asked, "Why are you here? Why are you Christians helping us? Where are our Arab brothers? Where is Saudi Arabia...Dubai?" Why should I be surprised? When we demonstrate the love of Jesus, we earn the right to share the reason why.

3. Conversion. Many people will experience serving in mission as their primary pathway to conversion. Serving will precede the more traditional pathways of worship attendance, Bible study groups, profession of faith, baptism, and membership. Many medical professionals have served multiple times in our Jamaican clinics, some up to four weeks a year. Some have connected to Bible studies and cell groups as a result of their mission experience. Others have begun to attend worship celebrations. A number remain unchurched. But all are experiencing the church and the mission of Jesus in a more positive light.

Jesus said that the world would know we were his disciples through the demonstration of his sacrificial love. The Western world has grown weary of the Christian church's hypocritical words, angry judgments, and nonresponsive action in the face of human need, injustice, and alarming environmental changes. Statistics from 2007 revealed that 37.3 million Americans were living in poverty (12.5 percent): 13.3 million children under the age of eighteen (18 percent) were in poverty; 3.6 million seniors aged sixty-five and older (9.7 percent) were in poverty; and 3.9 million

U.S. households (3.4 percent) accessed emergency food from a food pantry one or more times.[3] And what is Jesus' mission in the world?

> The Spirit of the Lord is upon me,
>   because he has anointed me
>   to bring good news to the poor.
> He has sent me to proclaim release to the captives
>   and recovery of sight to the blind,
>   to let the oppressed go free,
> to proclaim the year of the Lord's favor.
>   (Luke 4:18-19 NRSV)

If it is not good news for the poor, Church, it's not the gospel!

Questions for Reflection

1. Rate how efficiently you are using your current church facilities.
2. If someone totally unfamiliar with your church examined your budget, what would he or she conclude about your church's priorities?
3. What missional endeavor would you dream of accomplishing if your church suddenly paid off its entire mortgage? What changes can you make now that would enable you to follow God to that mission?

CHAPTER SEVEN

COURAGE VS. COMPLIANCE

Courage is being scared to death and saddling up anyway.
—*John Wayne*

At the heart of every decision we make about the future and purpose of the church is a choice between courage and compliance. Will we boldly take the difficult road and challenge people to go beyond their comfort zones into the places of Christ's calling? Or will we settle for what has always been, bowing to the wishes of the timid resisters?

Historians will identify the post-9/11 environment as an age of anxiety. Fear is an irrational emotion based on current circumstances or perceived future events. Reactive responses that result from these unchecked emotions can cause us to act outside our moral ideals. America's invasion of Iraq based on the perception of weapons of mass destruction or the use of torture as a means of extracting information from suspected terrorists are two examples of American actions that could not have occurred apart from the levels of anxiety created by the terrorist attacks of 9/11.

Just take a look at the economic factors that have fueled emotional levels of anxiety. The instability of oil prices can create the rise and fall of a barrel of crude by more than $100 in just a few months. In August of 2008 it cost me $70 to fill my tank, and by December, I could fill it for $27. The worldwide banking system nearly collapsed in 2008 based on the failures of some of the largest global banks and investment companies. The number of people finding themselves unemployed rose rapidly, fueled by the bankruptcies, buyouts, and closings of Fortune 500 companies and the resulting future tax burden created by the largest government bailout in history. The number of U.S. home foreclosures grew by 24 percent during the first three months of 2009 and continue to rise. Economists are using the scary *D* word as a future possibility. We are waking up to the reality that the Great Depression experienced by our grandparents might have been only the prelude to an apocalyptic global tomorrow.

The instability of the global political climate intensifies the human tendency to seek refuge in the security of our emotional and ideological fortresses. The boarding process at any airport accompanied by the graded levels of alert is a constant reminder of the possibility of attack. Nuclear proliferation in North Korea and Iran and the growth of militant Islam and its spread in the Western world can lead us as followers of Jesus to place our trust in the militant means of "chariots and horses" instead of the Lord our God. Fear creates a spirit of isolation that can lead the church to be more partisan and nationalistic than Christian. We also must guard against the tendency to allow fearful emotions due to the current global economic climate to insulate us from the plights and injustices experienced by the poor. The International Labor Organization estimates that more than 2.7 million people are being held in slavery throughout the world. I witnessed the atrocities of human trafficking when I visited Darfur in 2005. The Dinka people, who were forced to flee their homes during the twenty-year civil war in southern Sudan, had settled in the region of south Darfur. They were farmers without land or means to provide for their families. Surrendering their children to the Muslim landowners as indentured servants was the only means of survival for their children. With no financial resources to rent land and purchase seed and tools, the ability of the Dinka farmers to buy their children out of slavery seemed hopeless. Ginghamsburg Church's proactive response through the initiation of the Sudan Project in 2004 provided agricultural resources and training for 5,209 displaced families, which produced a fifteenfold return on the investment. This allowed the Dinka farmers to buy back 900 children!

Life is brief and fleeting. I am writing this chapter in the month of my thirtieth anniversary since coming to Ginghamsburg Church. It seems that it was just two or three years ago. In my trips around the country I occasionally run into friends and acquaintances whom I haven't seen since my seminary days. Isn't it amazing how people change in physical appearance from their middle twenties to late fifties? Especially when we haven't seen each other in thirty-plus years. Life is short! There is a cemetery behind my house where I regularly take contemplative walks with my dog. I look at the tombstones and wonder about the lives and stories of the people whose lifetimes are simply marked by the years of birth and death. My walks through the cemetery are reminders of both the gift and the brevity of life, and bring the realization that life is really defined by the dash between the two dates. Your life is a gift from God. It is what each of us does in the dash that becomes our gift back to God. Fear and anxiety can neutralize your opportunity to finish the unique role that you have been created to fulfill in your lifetime. We are all here to serve a purpose in God's redemptive mission. Don't waste the gift. There are no comebacks or do-overs. Your time is now!

God calls his people to act courageously in times of chaos. The children of God had allowed the paralysis of fear to turn what should have been an exodus trip of a few months into a forty-year waste of a lifetime for a whole generation. When Joshua was preparing to lead the new generation into the land of God's promise, here is what God said to him:

> Be strong and courageous; for you shall put this people in possession of the land that I swore to their ancestors to give them. Only be strong and very courageous, being careful to act in accordance with all the law that my servant Moses commanded you; do not turn from it to the right hand or to the left, so that you may be successful wherever you go. (Josh 1:6-7 NRSV)

There is an important lesson here for all of us who are entrusted with leadership in God's church. Don't follow the lead of the negative resisters or you will be buried in the wilderness with them! For too long I have witnessed cowardice in church leaders who allow the mean-spiritedness and faithlessness of the few to negate the mandates and purposes of God. Lyle Schaller once shared with me that Christlike character is the first quality needed in church staff and leadership. I would add to that Christlike courage!

Acting in Faith

The first words of Easter morning from the lips of our resurrected and reigning Lord were, "Do not be afraid." Faith is not the absence of fear. Faith is feeling the fear and then acting on the promises and purpose of God anyway. Faith is when every cell in your body is screaming, "Run!" while you continue to follow forward in obedience, praying, "Not my will, Lord, but your will be done!" Faith is the proactive response, in spite of those feelings and uncertainties, to the mandates of heaven.

Mother Teresa is one of the best testaments to the reality of Jesus' presence in the world that I have witnessed in my lifetime, but few knew that she had experienced a sense of "the absence of the presence of God" for almost her entire ministry.[1] She spent her first years as a nun teaching in parochial schools. She noted having an experience in 1946 when Christ spoke to her and said, "Come be my light to the poorest of the poor." She devoted the next two years to prayerfully seeking the counsel of her superiors and formulating a mission strategy. In 1948 she founded the Missionaries of Charity and began to minister to the poorest of the poor in the streets of Calcutta. From 1948 until her death in 1997 she felt that Jesus' presence had abandoned her. In her letters to her confessors she referred to Jesus as "The Great Absent One" and stated that it seemed his relationship to her was like "the comatose spouse." In 1953 she wrote to her confessor: "Please pray for me that I may not spoil his work and that our Lord may show himself—for there is such terrible darkness within me, as if everything was dead. It has been like this more or less from the time I started the work." For forty-nine years, except for a brief five-week period she mentioned in 1959, one of the greatest missionaries of all time felt the absence of God's presence. Can you imagine the hole that would be left in the fabric of the world if Mother Teresa had acted on her feelings rather than the mandate of the gospel? The absence of feeling does not mean the absence of God. Feelings are not required for faith and may be misleading. Faith is not the absence of doubt or fear. Faith is acting on God's word in spite of!

I find four directives for faith given by Jesus after his resurrection to be extremely practical for leadership in chaotic times of uncertainty (see Matt 28).

1. *Don't let fear determine your actions.* When Jesus told the women not to fear, he was saying in effect, "Don't allow irrational emotion to determine your course of action; rather, act on the promise of God." God is the God of abundance, love, life, and provision. Not even death can deny God's redemptive plan. No circumstance can change the promise or purposes of God! Life is a choice. We choose our life situation. God said, "I have set before you life and death, blessings and curses. Now choose life, so that you and your children may live" (Deut 30:19). To experience life, you must take risks. One of my favorite biblical stories is about Peter when he stepped out of the boat and attempted to walk on water. There wasn't anything about the act that made sense. Others saw it as rash and impulsive. When he began to sink, I'm sure there were plenty of "I told you so's" and "I knew the fool was crazy." Why did Peter do it? Peter stepped out of the boat because he heard Jesus say, "Come!" Like the eleven disciples who stayed in the boat, most will miss the wonder of a miraculous life mission because they will never act beyond the confines of the lifeboat or outside the expectations of those traveling with them. And might I add that we have learned to insulate ourselves as the church in some pretty comfortable self-contained lifeboats—or cruise ships, as we discussed in chapter 1!

If you allow fear to determine your decisions and actions, you will lose your life. Why do people stay in destructive, abusive relationships? Why do people stay in jobs they hate instead of taking the risks to pursue a lifelong passion? Why do pastors allow un-Christlike decisions to prevail on church boards and councils? Why don't people stand up and speak out and act in the face of injustice? It all comes down to one word—*fear*. That was why the first words out of Jesus' mouth after the resurrection were, "Do not be afraid!" There is no circumstance, world leader, or even church board that can derail the righteous purpose of God. The purpose of God for a time might be delayed, but it will not be denied. God will have the last word! Faith is persistently hoping in God's promised outcome and committing to the resulting actions to achieve that outcome.

2. *Recognize holy ground.* The women came to the tomb expecting to find a corpse and instead witnessed a world-changing miracle: "The angel said to the women, 'Do not be afraid; I know that you are looking for Jesus who was crucified. He is not here; for he has been raised, as he said. Come, see the place where he lay'" (Matt 28:5-6 NRSV). Now the place where he had been laid was a cemetery. What do you expect to find in a cemetery—death? God does his best work in places of death. God's people need to camp right in the middle of the Darfurs of this world and plant churches in blighted urban areas.

I have discovered that the fruit of a person's life work rise to the level of his or her expectations. "As he thinketh in his heart, so is he" (Prov 23:7 KJV). I hear many church leaders bemoan the fact that they can't begin to have anywhere near the impact of a church like Ginghamsburg because of their church size, location, resistant people, and lack of resources. You have heard all of the "can't because" excuses and can probably add a few more of your own. Don't forget that Ginghamsburg is located in a community of twenty-two houses, sixteen miles north of one of the ten fastest dying cities in the United States. The population has declined during my thirty-plus-year tenure. There were fewer than one hundred people in the church when I arrived and thirty left that first year. I inherited a $27,000 budget, I was met with resistance, and I still have days when I feel like throwing in the towel. During those times, I remind myself that God does his best work in desperate situations. You don't need different circumstances, new surroundings, a different spouse, or more resources. You are in God's place, in God's time. Wherever you are, God is.

Jacob had a dream in which God promised to "bless the land on which he was lying." When he woke up, he said, "Surely the LORD is in this place, and I was not aware of it. . . . How awesome is this place! This is none other than the house of God; this is the gate of heaven" (Gen 28:16-17). Remember Joseph, who was thrown into a pit and sold into slavery? It seemed that this good guy was always getting the short end of the stick. Yet "the LORD was with Joseph, and he became a successful man" (Gen 39:2 NRSV). Both men were standing in God's place in God's time. It is time to wake up, Church. For surely God is in this place. We are standing at the gate of heaven to be the conduit of heaven's resources for the least and the lost. You don't need to be in a different place, my sisters and brothers. The place where you are standing is holy ground!

3. *Serve God's purpose in others.* Jesus told the women, "Do not be afraid," and then, "Go and tell my brothers to go to Galilee; there they will see me" (Matt 28:10). How do we witness to the reality of the resurrection? How will others see? Jesus stated, "I give you a new commandment, that you love one another. Just as I have loved you, you also should love one another. By this everyone will know that you are my disciples, if you have love for one another" (John 13:34-35 NRSV). Jesus wasn't referring to an emotional, warm fuzzy feeling kind of love but a sacrificial laying down of our lives and resources for the world for which Jesus gave his. How do we serve Jesus? We serve him by enacting heaven's purpose in the lives of the oppressed and marginalized. And we believe what he said: "Truly I tell you, just as you did it to one of the least of these who are members of my family, you did it to me" (Matt 25:40 NRSV). How are you serving Jesus by serving others, especially those on the margins of society?

I had the opportunity to sit down and interview John Prendergast, cofounder of the Enough Project. John has spent twenty-five years of his life working in African war zones. He served as an official in the Clinton White House. After leaving that position, he realized that we could never do enough to stop crimes against

humanity and work for peace without involving larger con-
stituencies of people. John had come to Ginghamsburg to be part
of a live CCN (Church Communication Network) satellite broad-
cast to churches gathered together throughout North America to
better understand the church's role in stopping genocide in the
world. The program was called "Not on Our Watch." John had
coauthored the book by the same title with the actor Don Chea-
dle. After the program, we sat together in my office and talked
about John's Christian faith and how it has influenced his role as
an activist, in which he gives his life to educate and mobilize people to work to alleviate crimes committed against humanity. I
asked John for an example of where the church has made a difference. This is what he said:

> This has been perhaps one of the most dramatic success stories
> in the last twenty years. From the beginning of his presidency,
> President [George W.] Bush heard that Sudan mattered to
> Christian constituencies all across the United States. Bush ap-
> pointed former Senator Jack Danforth, an ordained Episcopal
> Priest, in 2001, as US special envoy to Sudan. Over 2 million
> people in Southern Sudan had died in the civil war that had
> gone on for twenty years. Senator Danforth provide direction to
> a peace team that represented a coalition of nations. He sup-
> ported a peace deal that officially ended the civil war between
> Sudan's Islamist government and Sudanese Rebels from the
> partly Christian South. This shows the positive influence of the
> church and the power of American diplomacy.

Praise God for the people of God who stand in courage and
speak to evil in Jesus' name, "Not on our watch!"

God never intended for people to sit around and wait for
heaven. Jesus calls us from our complacency and places of comfort
to go into all the world and make disciples. This calling is not just
for professional clergy but also for every person who responds to
Jesus' invitation, "Follow me!" Tom and Elaine Sampley have been
part of Ginghamsburg Church's ministry longer than I have. They
were part of the very first discipleship group that Carolyn and I had
in our home when we came to Ginghamsburg in 1979. Tom was a

successful business owner living a comfortable lifestyle when he and Elaine received an Abraham type of calling: "Go from your country and your kindred and your father's house to the land that I will show you" (Gen 12:1 NRSV). Tom and Elaine, empty nesters in their midfifties, picked up and moved to the Czech Republic to begin a mission outreach to atheists. They opened a coffee shop that they named Common Grounds, the same name that we use for our coffee shop at Ginghamsburg. They built relationships with people in the community while they held business seminars and taught English classes, using the Bible as the textbook. After eight years of faithful labor and now in their midsixties, they were able to plant a church. Tom e-mailed me recently:

> Yesterday was a great day of celebration. Petra was baptized in the cold Berounka River near our house. Our fellowship gathered on the bank. I read from the scriptures in Romans on being dead to sin and alive in Christ symbolized by baptism. Petra celebrated her new walk with Jesus in front of many witnesses from our body of Christ gathered along the shoreline. Petra gave testimony of her journey to believe in Jesus. She cited the influence of Common Grounds people along the way and a Common Grounds retreat five years ago in the mountains. That's when Jackie from Ginghamsburg joined our team here in the Czech Republic. God brought Jackie into Petra's life to love her and share God's love with her. She met other people who came from Ginghamsburg each summer to help lead our English Camp. Another member of Ginghamsburg Church shared his life at the camp and then later by email challenged Petra to believe. When she arrived back home in Revnice, she began to go online and listen to Ginghamsburg's Sunday messages. So now the Lord has brought us six people this year who have been baptized and regularly join the fellowship of over 40 people celebrating Jesus each Sunday.

How can we change the world? By equipping disciples, some in small out-of-the-way places like Ginghamsburg, who will go into the world and serve God's purpose in others.

4. *Focus forward.* Jesus is always moving ahead of the church

into the future. We will never find God's purpose in the "good old days" of the past or in "that's the way we've always done it." Don't look back. God's best days are before us. Lot's wife looked back, and she turned into a pillar of salt. Her longing for the security and traditions of the past sucked the life right out of her. "Faith is the assurance of things hoped for, the conviction of things not seen" (Heb 11:1 NRSV). God's purpose is in front of us—never behind. Don't look back or allow yourself to become too comfortable in the present.

Continue to Pioneer into God's Future

Helping people see the simple truth of Jesus' purpose. Reconnecting women and men to the basic message and mission of Jesus. This is when real change begins in a local church. And this Holy Spirit–empowered change becomes a contagion that spreads through communities and ultimately the world!

Leading change requires the movement leader to be strategically focused. In my first year at Ginghamsburg, I took a threefold approach. First, I taught from the pulpit each week about the nature and character of the church's mission, using the book of Acts as the text. Next, it was important that I right-size the organization by creating a simpler board structure and eliminating the majority of traditional church committees. I also moved all of the committee meetings to the same night. Instead of spending their time in meetings, people were released to grow healthy families and serve the community. After all, people are seeking significance—not more meetings. The final focus for establishing the missional DNA that first year was putting a leadership development process in place that would replicate the life and mission of Jesus in others.[2] I knew that I could never change the resisters; I needed to form my own new teams. I had to grow the people who would become the biblical Joshuas and Deborahs to lead this new missional movement, and I had to ensure that they were placed in positions of influence and authority.

I'm often asked how I was able to remove from authority the resisters, the "godmothers" and "godfathers" of the church who were firmly entrenched in long-held committee positions, effectively creating barriers to forward progress. We are a United Methodist church, and our Book of Discipline requires that representatives on key committees take a sabbatical from those positions after three years of service. I ensured that the Discipline was enforced, for the first time in many years. (To my United Methodist colleagues, the Discipline also gives you the flexibility to reorganize your structure if changes in membership size, program scope, mission resources, or other circumstances require it, provided that the plan is approved by your district superintendent.[3] This is a great opportunity to pour new wine into new wineskins.) Even if your church's governance does not require leadership transitions, I recommend that you make a "three-year rule" one of the first orders of business for your board, emphasizing how important it is to include fresh faces and fresh ideas in ministry decisions and visioning.

Instilling the missional DNA requires bold steps. In 1979, after two months of convincing the board, we opened our little country church for a weekly Alcoholics Anonymous meeting. At that time, to host AA meetings, you had to be willing to permit attendees to smoke cigarettes and drink coffee in the meeting space—not something you should do in a church! But when I stood on the platform each Sunday preaching and saw the cigarette burns in the carpet before me, I knew that we were becoming the people of Jesus. Maybe this is why we remain a "recovery" church to this day.

Ultimately, you must be a confident and courageous leader who says and does the hard things to ensure the success of the mission. A student recently told me in a seminary class I was leading that she had heard I was cocky but she had found me instead to be confident. I am confident—not in my own abilities—but confident because of the Christ who calls me and the Christ who lives in me.

Christmas Is Not Your Birthday

Christmas Day has become the number one self-focused consumer day in America. The indicator of its economic success is determined by the day after Thanksgiving sales, appropriately named Black Friday. This ominous name seems even more appropriate after a Long Island Wal-Mart store employee was crushed to death in the stampede of early morning shoppers in November 2008. A group of churches has been leading a movement in recent years called the Advent Conspiracy to challenge this hedonistic focus.

Since 2004, the folks at Ginghamsburg have tried to reframe the message and mission of Christmas as being Christ's birthday and to do what honors him on the occasion of his birth. Christmas is not about us! We have chosen to make the Advent season a focus on the Sudan Project and to sacrificially raise the needed funds for the coming year. We spend minimally on our families so that we can give sacrificially for the needs of people in Darfur. We build the Christmas Eve celebrations around this mission focus. Many people would not consider this to be a seeker-friendly marketing strategy on what has become the highest attendance day of the year. Churches tend to market the day to appeal to the feel-good traditions of the season. And I agree that there will be those who are turned off by Ginghamsburg's annual appeal to self-sacrifice in order to benefit African refugees. In the middle of December I received from a past Christmas Eve attendee the following e-mail, which shows just how caught up we get in the prevailing secular expectation and miss the real meaning:

> Mr. Slaughter,
> Thank you for allowing my family to enjoy the great Christmas services at your church over the last many years. You are a gifted speaker I greatly enjoy listening to.
> I'm sorry to say that although I understand the great work that needs to be done, and the work you've already accomplished, I simply can't take another African Christmas. I hope this doesn't sound harsh, but our Christmas celebration is not limited to Africa year after year. So this year we will gather in hopes of finding a new worship spot that is more traditional to the Christmas we know.

The traditional Christmas that we have grown up with is about a feel-good, insulated, holly-jolly Santa Claus Jesus who leaves us isolated from the needs of the world. We are detached from the servant Son of God who would not be exempt or insulated from pain, suffering, or death. Jesus experienced the injustice and unfairness of life in its extremes when, beginning at age two, he lived with his family as refugees in Africa to escape the Judean genocide. He was executed as a criminal of the state around the age of thirty-three. So will someone please tell me: Where is the disconnect between Jesus' birthday, refugees, genocide, and Africa?

The church has been compliant far too long. We have stood by silently and closed our eyes in indifference. We have participated in the atrocities of evil simply in our refusal to speak or act.

The contemporary church has tended to err either by denying the validity of the uniqueness of Jesus and the historicity of his resurrection or by retreating into a form of the ancient cult of Gnosticism, which regards God's creation as inherently evil and seeks refuge in a future disembodied heaven. The Bible teaches not about some form of disembodied heaven after death but about the resurrection of the body and the creation of a new heaven and earth. God has not abandoned the planet or the people in it. God is constantly restoring, renewing, redeeming, and resurrecting. The people of Jesus are called to be a counterculture community who are demonstrating heaven's purpose on earth.

I have used parts of Len's Sweet's "Magna Carta of Trust by an Out-of-Control Disciple" as a congregational declaration of faith in worship. Renewals and reformation are never born out of timidity. I love to "double dare" women and men to live beyond the limits of reason and to grab hold of God's possibilities through limitless faith. Consider Sweet's words:

> I am part of the Church of the Out-of-Control. I once was a control junkie, but now am an Out-of-Control Disciple. I've given up my control to God. I trust and obey the Spirit. I've jumped off the fence, I've stepped over the line, I've pulled out all the stops, I'm holding nothing back. There's no turning back, looking around, slowing down, backing away, letting up, or shutting up. It's life Against the Odds, Outside the Box, Over the Wall, the game of life played Without Goal Lines other than "Thy Will Be Done..."
>
> I'm done lapdogging for the topdogs, the wonderdogs, the overdogs, or even the underdogs. I'm done playing According to the Rules, whether it's Robert's Rules of Order or Miss Manners' Rules of Etiquette or Martha Stewart's Rules of Living or Louis

Farrakhan's Rules of America's Least Wanted or Merrill Lynch's Money-minding/Bottom-lining/Ladder-climbing Rules of America's Most Wanted.

I am not here to please the dominant culture or to serve any all-show/no-go bureaucracies. I live to please my Lord and Savior. My spiritual taste-buds have graduated from fizz and froth to Fire and Ice. Sometimes I'm called to sharpen the cutting edge, and sometimes to blunt the cutting edge. Don't give me that old-time religion. Don't give me that new-time religion. Give me that all-time religion that's as hard as rock and as soft as snow.

I've stopped trying to make life work, and started trying to make life sing. I'm finished with second-hand sensations, third-rate dreams, low-risk high-rise trades and goose-stepping, flag-waving crusades. I no longer live by and for anything but everything God-breathed, Christ-centered, and Spirit-driven.

The church is called to be out of control! Such a mind-set characterized the spread and controversial impact of the first-century church. Incredible numbers of people were committing to the movement, and many were violently attacking it. In Thessalonica, mobs attacked believers meeting in Jason's house and dragged Jason out, shouting, "These people who have been turning the world upside down have come here also" (Acts 17:6 NRSV).

You and I are called to be part of a world-changing, Spirit-empowered "hell can't prevail" community of action. The outcome will not be determined by the size of your congregation or the abundance of your resources—only your willingness to leave the safety of your life raft and the compliance of those who choose to remain on it. Have courage, Saints—for God is in this place and the gates of hell cannot prevail against us!

Questions for Reflection
1. What anxieties or fears are standing in the way of your acting out in faith?
2. Do you recognize the holy ground on which you are already standing? What is God calling you to do there?
3. If you let yourself get "out of control," what could God do through you?

NOTES

Introduction

1. See "America's Fastest-Dying Cities" by Joshua Zumbrun, *Forbes*, http://www.forbes.com/2008/08/04/economy-ohio-michigan-biz_cx_jz_0805dying.html.

2. Ibid.

3. David Kinnaman and Gabe Lyons, *Unchristian: What a New Generation Really Thinks about Christianity* (Grand Rapids: Baker Books, 2007), 24, 27.

4. See www.americanreligionsurvey-aris.org.

5. Kinnaman and Lyons, 24, 27.

6. Lovett Weems presented these statistics to a gathering of pastors from the ten largest UMC churches in Houston, Texas, February 12, 2009.

7. Scott Thuma and Dave Travis, *Beyond Megachurch Myths: What We Can Learn from America's Largest Churches* (San Francisco: Jossey-Bass, 2007), 1.

8. My book *UnLearning Church* (Nashville: Abingdon Press, 2008) discusses this transition from an ABC-focused ministry to a ministry that mobilizes modern people to do the work of Jesus in the world today.

1. Missional vs. Attractional

1. Scott Elliot, "Outlook for Levy Grim in Dayton," *Dayton Daily News*, June 3, 2008.

2. See http://www.unicef.org/sowc05/english/povertyissue2.html.

3. From his work *The Church as the People of God*. I took it from Alan Hirsch's *Forgotten Ways* (Grand Rapids: Brazos Press, 2007), 15.

4. David Kinnaman and Gabe Lyons, *Unchristian: What a New*

Generation Really Thinks about Christianity (Grand Rapids: Baker Books, 2007), 15.

3. Disciples vs. Decisions

1. For more on this subject, I recommend that you check out N. T. Wright's book *Surprised by Hope: Rethinking Heaven, the Resurrection, and the Mission of the Church* (New York: HarperOne, 2008). Wright challenges us to rethink faith with a holistic understanding of resurrection.

2. This curriculum by Carolyn Slaughter is available from Abingdon Press under the title *Following Jesus: Steps to a Passionate Faith* (Nashville: Abingdon Press, 2008).

3. Mother Teresa, *Jesus Is My All in All: Praying with the "Saint of Calcutta,"* ed. Brian Kolodiejchuk (New York: Doubleday, 2008), 43.

4. Wikipedia, "Imprinting." http://en.wikipedia.org/wiki/Imprinting_ (psychology)

5. Ginghamsburg's discipleship tools, including *Transformation Journal* and *Following Jesus,* are available at www.ginghamsburg.org/conferencesandbooks.

6. Alan Hirsch, *The Forgotten Ways* (Grand Rapids: Brazos Press, 2007), 122.

4. Micro vs. Macro

1. David Kinnaman, "Speaking a New Language of Spirituality," *Rev! Magazine* (Jan.-Feb. 2009): 16.

2. Thom S. Rainer and Eric Geiger, *Simple Church: Returning to God's Process for Making Disciples* (Nashville: Broadman Press, 2006) 14, 60.

3. Donald Miller, *Blue Like Jazz: Nonreligious Thoughts on Christian Spirituality* (Nashville: Thomas Nelson, 2003) 132-36.

4. Frank Viola and George Barna, *Pagan Christianity?: Exploring the Roots of Our Church Practices* (Carol Stream, Ill.: BarnaBooks, 2007), 14-15, 18.

5. Multiplication vs. Expansion

1. See my book *Momentum for Life* (Nashville: Abingdon Press, 2008).

2. See http://www.artukraine.com/old/historical/lenin_makeover.htm.

3. Howard Snyder, *The Community of the King,* rev. ed., 2nd ed. (Downers Grove, Ill.: InterVarsity Press, 2004), 123.

4. Rom 16:5; 1 Cor 16:19; Col 4:15; Phlm 2. See Howard Snyder's chapter on church growth and kingdom growth in *The Community of the King.*

5. Snyder, 123.

6. Mark Galli, "Glocal Church Ministry," *Christianity Today* interview, posted August 2, 2007.

7. See statehealthfacts.org.

8. "Rethink Church" is the UMC's newest advertising campaign, launched in May 2009.

9. Great African American churches were the exception to this rule. Windsor Village United Methodist Church and St. John's Downtown Church, both in Houston, and Trinity United Church of Christ in Chicago are examples of megachurches caring for the least of these in major urban areas.

6. Mission vs. Mortar

1. Howard Snyder, *The Problem of Wine Skins* (Downers Grove, Ill.: InterVarsity Press, 1975), 69.

2. Check out Kim's book *Redesigning Worship* (Nashville: Abingdon Press, 2009) for insights on creating inspiring, engaging worship experiences on a budget.

3. See Feeding America, http://feedingamerica.org/faces-of-hunger/hunger-101/hunger-and-poverty-statistics.aspx.

7. Courage vs. Compliance

1. Read Mother Teresa's *Come Be My Light: The Private Writings of the "Saint of Calcutta,"* ed. Brian Kolodiejchuk (New York: Doubleday, 2007). for more about the absence of God that she felt.

2. For more on the subject of leading bold change, see my book *Spiritual Entrepreneurs* (Nashville: Abingdon Press, 1994).

3. *The Book of Discipline of The United Methodist Church* (Nashville: United Methodist Publishing House, 2008), ¶247.

RETHINK CHURCH

Rethink Church is a movement designed to remind those inside and outside of faith communities that church is not just a place we go, but something we do. Created by the people of The United Methodist Church, it presents doorways to spirituality–everything from global health initiatives to daycare and sports programs.

Resources for United Methodist congregations and conferences: www.rethinkchurch.org

For those looking for their doorway to changing the world: www.10thousanddoors.org